THE REBIRTH OF A NATION

The uncommon man

I do not choose to be a common man. It is my right to be uncommon if I can. I seek opportunity — not security. I do not wish to be a kept citizen, humbled and dulled by having the state look after me. I want to take the calculated risk; to dream and to build, to fail and to succeed. I refuse to barter incentive for a dole. I prefer the challenges of life to the guaranteed existence; the thrill of fulfillment to the stale calm of Utopia. I will not trade freedom for beneficence, nor my dignity for a handout. I will never cower before any master nor bend to any threat. It is my heritage to stand erect, proud and unafraid; to think and act for myself, enjoy the benefits of my creations and to face the world boldly and say, 'this I have done'!
All this is what being an American means to me.

— Dean Alfange

THE REBIRTH OF A NATION

WITH A BILL OF RIGHTS FOR AMERICA'S THIRD CENTURY

CONCEIVED AND EDITED BY ROBERT S. MINOR

DESIGNED BY MARINUS WELMAN

Published by Third Century Fund
a division of National Heritage Foundation

★ THE CAST

FOREWORD
By RONALD REAGAN

THE COMING BREAKPOINT
By SENATOR BARRY GOLDWATER

CAMEOS BY;
MARJORIE W. FLUOR

JOHN WAYNE

CARL N. KARCHER

U.S. SENATOR HARRY F. BYRD, JR.

LAWRENCE WELK

WARREN T. BROOKES

U.S. REP. PHILIP M. CRANE

JOSEPH T. BAILEY

U.S. SENATOR JAMES B. ALLEN

DR. ROBERT H. SCHULLER

DR. ARTHUR F. BURNS

ACKNOWLEDGEMENTS

Grateful acknowledgement is made to
Governor Ronald Reagan, Marjorie Fluor,
John Wayne, Carl Karcher, U.S. Senator
Harry F. Byrd, Jr., Lawrence Welk,
Warren T. Brookes, Congressman Philip
Crane, Joseph T. Bailey, U.S. Senator James
B. Allen and Dr. Robert Schuller for their
eloquent messages herein and to . . .

Macmillan Publishing Company and
Senator Barry Goldwater for permission
to reprint a condensation of his book,
"The Coming Breakpoint" and to . . .

The Warner & Swasey Company for
permission to reprint a selection of their
stirring messages about what America
has been, and can be again, which have
appeared in leading national publications
over more than forty years, and to . . .

Dr. Arnold O. Beckman, the C.C. Chapman
Foundation, Kathleen Crow, Robert
Guggenheim, Peter Hannaford, Clarence
Hoiles, Peter G. Muth, H. Bruce Palmer,
Dr. Robert Peterson, Ward Ritchie, James
C. Roberts, Jerry Roberts, Jack and Valerie
Scudder, Frank and Olga Schroeder, Dr.
Robert F. Williams and Charles Hull Wolfe
for their invaluable aid and advice in the
development of this book, and especially
to Carl Karcher, Don McBride and Adolf
Schoepe for their support in making this
first printing possible.

R.S.M.

EDITOR'S NOTE

Nearly two centuries ago, British Historian Alexander Tyler, writing of the collapse of those great democracies—ancient Athens and Rome, warned:

"A democracy cannot exist as a permanent form of government. It can exist only until the voters discover they can vote themselves largess out of the public treasury. From that moment on, the majority always votes for the candidate promising the most benefits from the public treasury—with the result that democracy collapses under the weight of a loose fiscal policy. Always to be followed by a dictatorship."

Frightening words for Americans who have been taught that we invented democracy and, in so doing, placed ourselves beyond the reach of despotism forever more—never mind that we fail to elect fiscally responsible people with the integrity to say NO to our "freebee" appetites. We have not been heeding the few heroic leaders of the day who are telling us how we are sowing the same seeds of self-destruction that brought down other slothful democracies of the past. As Senator Goldwater emphatically affirms in his recent book, THE COMING BREAKPOINT (condensed herein—Section I) "What is past is prologue.—study the past!"

Pre-dating the publication of this book were many months of search and inquiry as to how best portray:

(1) The way the American spirit of self-reliance is being surrendered to ever-increasing dependency on government—with the people looking to the state to solve all their problems, when it cannot even solve its own.

(2) The zeal with which the world's most massive bureaucracy seeks to seize total control of the people's affairs, its equally massive failures and costs in so doing—

and with ruinous inflation as the first visible punishment that the people must endure.

(3) The ultimate price—national bankruptcy and the loss of liberty, unless we soon change our ways.

Involved in the search were refreshing conversations with educators, economists, publicists, and leaders in business and political life. A composite of the harvest of those conversations may well be stated by a letter from one savant which included the following:

"I enjoyed our chat and presentation of your proposed book. It is certainly a fascinating idea. Any work dealing with economics tends to turn people off from pursuing the subject to any length. And yet, the economic facts of life, and their treatment by government, determine the fortunes, the happiness, and the liberties of us all.

"The best way to capture the interest of the uninformed and misinformed masses is to give them the message in a simple and articulate form, encased in a dramatic format. I have found it very difficult to find such a presentation—one that people would really enjoy reading and, with some eagerness, pass on, one to another. Your proposed book, "The Rebirth of a Nation," featuring the celebrated Warner & Swasey editorials, may be just the thing to fill this urgent need."

In essence, that passage expresses the intent, and the hope, that underlie the conception and publication of this book.

Robert S. Minor

"Posterity, you will never know how much
it has cost my generation to preserve your
freedom. I hope you will make good use of it."

— John Quincy Adams

DEDICATED TO THOSE GALLANT
EDUCATORS AND LIBERTY LOVING
YOUTH WHOSE CO-SEARCH FOR
TRUTH SHALL LEAD TO A SOLVENT
AMERICA AND A REBIRTH
OF FREEDOM IN OUR LAND.

and to Adelaide

CONTENTS:

A BILL OF RIGHTS FOR

AMERICA'S THIRD CENTURY

ABOUT RONALD REAGAN

Ronald Reagan has said, "I am not a professional politician. I am a citizen with a deep seated belief that much of what troubles us has been brought about by politicians . . . playing upon the economic illiteracy of the American people."

He believes that never has there been a greater need for an informed citizenry, and never has there been a greater lack of awareness of how our system works.

But his gift for dramatizing and articulating the reasons for the nation's woes is making its impact. Thanks to him people are beginning to understand the causes behind persistent inflation, and the cost to them of constant deficit spending, mounting federal debt, bureaucracy, waste and boondoggles and federal over-regulation—all of which leads to the loss of liberty. They are saying, "it wasn't this way 20 years ago—why must it be now? What went wrong?"

May Ronald Reagan continue his crusade for a better understanding of the nation's ills and what is going on in Washington that only the people themselves can correct.

FOREWORD

By RONALD REAGAN

On the pages that follow you will read much about freedom and about government.

The nature of freedom is that it is fragile. It must be protected, watched over, sometimes fought over.

The nature of government is that it will grow and grow and grow. That is, it will if it is not restrained, watched over and its actions constantly reviewed and appraised.

Those who turn to government to solve problems best left to individuals, families and communities are probably unaware that their actions combine with those of countless others to encourage government to do things the Founding Fathers never intended it to do. And, in striving to be all things to all people, government can acquire the means to suffocate freedom.

Our nation has begun its third century. The United States of America—a noble experiment that has survived to be, in many respects, an example for others around the world to want to emulate. Nowhere have individual rights and freedoms been more highly prized than in these United States. But, the fundamental precept of the Founding Fathers of our republic that those who govern do so only with the consent of the governed is becoming distorted. As the federal government has swollen to gargantuan size, it has bred a layer of permanent rule-makers—the bureaucrats—who, more than the Congress, affect our daily lives by imposing countless rules and regulations. The more government has preempted the incomes of the people, the larger it has grown and the more it has interfered in the private business and private affairs of the American people.

A basic question facing us in this, our third century as a nation, is will we become a society ruled by elitists, or will we recapture the spirit of individual responsibility and initiative that brought us greatness and worldwide leadership?

Some among us insist that our society can become nearly perfect if only they be given the necessary controls to make the rest of us do what is "right." They will of course define "right" and "wrong" for us. Such matters are not to be left to the individual, the family, school or church— the traditional builders of values. No, values are to be decided in Washington, D.C. by high-minded idealists who will set down the rules of behavior.

That is not what the Founding Fathers intended. They sought to give to each person the opportunity to do the very best with whatever gifts God had endowed him—or her.

A nation faces risks and dangers in its dealings with other nations, but we face a danger within our own society as well. That is, that government will become so swollen, so pervasive, so all-powerful that the very meaning of our Constitution and Bill of Rights will be twisted beyond recognition.

Government itself can become the enemy within if it is allowed to have undue influence over our lives, threatening our basic freedom.

We must arm ourselves with the best tools we can to check its spreading power. The Constitution and the Bill of Rights are strong, well-hewn tools for this purpose.

The Fourth and Tenth Amendments of the Constitution, especially are being cited more and more by earnest, patriotic Americans intent on preserving individual freedoms and restraining government. The Fourth Amendment says that "The right of the people to be secure in their persons, houses, papers and effects against unreasonable searches and seizures shall not be violated." These days it is being used constructively to check and turn back arbitrary demands of some government agencies on private citizens and businesses.

The Tenth Amendment will come into play more and more in the coming years, I believe, as more and more Americans seek to reseize for themselves and their communities the initiative that has been allowed to pass to Washington. The Tenth Amendment reaffirms the fact that we are a federation of sovereign states. It says, "The powers not delegated to the United States by the Constitution, nor prohibited by it to the states, are reserved to the states respectively, or to the people."

In this book you will read about many dimensions of the growing struggle to reclaim the rights and responsibilities of individuals, families, communities and the states.

Here is a sampling of the subjects:

* The *right* to take action against the coming breakpoint in America.
* The *right* to hold our lawmakers accountable for the ravages of inflation.
* The *right* to be positive about freedom.
* The *right* of private enterprise to be free to produce the profits which create the new jobs that spawn prosperity for all.
* The *right* to choose liberty and individual achievement over the chains of the welfare state.
* The *right* to take action against the perils of government spending beyond the people's ability to pay.
* The *right* to invoke the 10th Amendment—restoration of governing powers reserved to the states and the people.
* The *right* to realization of the American Dream—sovereignty of the individual under God.

Introductions to these chapters have been written by a group of distinguished citizens from public and private life and from varying political backgrounds. They share one thing in common: deep concern for the future of our country. But they speak of hope, too: hope for a "Rebirth of a Nation"—a solvent America for the generations to come.

You play an important role in the American drama, too. Please read the important messages in this book about America's challenges and its opportunities. I know you will enjoy them. Then, join us; work—and pray—for our republic.

Ronald Reagan

"There is nothing on this earth more glorious than a man's freedom, and no aim more elevated than liberty"

—THOMAS PAINE
Entreaty to the Continental troops, 1775

ABOUT MARJORIE WADE FLUOR

A woman of deep sensibilities and wide-ranging humanitarian concerns, Marjorie Wade Fluor combines active philanthropic service in California with a career as a writer, and a licensed Practioner of Religious Science.

Wife of the late industrialist, J. Simon Fluor, she is the biographical author of *ALFRED NOBEL, THE LONELIEST MILLIONAIRE*, written with Michael Evlanoff and published in 1969 by Ward Ritchie Press. The Virginia born descendent of an original Jamestown settler, she now makes her home in Santa Ana, California.

Marjorie Fluor is a past Regent and past State Chaplain of the Daughters of the American Revolution; a leader in the World Affairs Council, Eastern Star, P.E.O. and the National League of American Pen Women.

A degree in Metaphysics and special research in the field of Religious Science reflect Mrs. Fluor's long-standing interest in comparative religions and psychic phenomena. Extensive business experience in property management reflects her understanding of American free enterprise.

Her profound concern for revealing the truth about the state of America's freedom under today's socialistic trends and pressures is expressed with powerful simplicity on the following page.

TRUTH—
THE GUARDIAN OF FREEDOM

By MARJORIE WADE FLUOR

200 years ago something new and wonderful happened to the world—the United States of America was born!

It was then that Thomas Paine, known as the voice of the American War for Independence, penned this stirring refrain:

"For such is the irresistible nature of truth that all it wishes, and all it needs, is the liberty of appearing."

By such words as these he sought to implant in the hearts of his countrymen the conviction that truth was their sword and their shield, and that oppression in any form cannot long prevail in truth's holy light.

As we now embark upon our third century as a republic, we find ourselves drifting into an acceptance of falsehoods in the arena of our political and economic behaviors, threatening the freedom for which our forefathers paid so dearly.

We are surrendering our basic American values and disciplines to the fantasy that there is a bottomless government treasure trove into which we can forever dip without having to work for or repay. We are permitting our majority representatives in Congress to spend 50, 60, and 70 billions of dollars a year more than we can provide in taxes, and thus forcing our government to print mountains of greenbacks to make up the difference. As those "greenbacks" have no underlying worth to fortify them, they dilute the value of all currency and thus become an especially cruel destroyer called inflation. We are rapidly learning that nothing is free.

Let us, then, cease our ever-increasing demands upon our debt ridden government and insist that those in power start facing and preaching some fundamental truths:

★ That no family, no community, no state, however compassionately motivated, can long indulge in spending beyond its income without courting disaster for all, including the recipients of their benevolent intents; and that this fact of life applies to a federation of states as well as to any component thereof.
★ That human wants are, and always will be, inexhaustible, while human resources to gratify them are not.
★ That government, uncontrolled, generates a constant self-growth thrust of power and debt which, if not halted, leads to the inevitable result that, in order to govern at all, it must become the master of the people, rather than the servant.
★ That there is always a price to be paid for whatever is received; that in order to have things they must first be produced; that government produces nothing, it only consumes, and that the more it consumes the less is left for those it governs.
★ That the price of continued deficit spending is a fire storm of inflation so unbearable that, as with other nations in our time, the people must turn their lives over to a ruling few to dictate what they can have, and what they can and cannot do, as the last resort to escape economic chaos.

I do believe that truth is our mightiest guardian of our freedom. And in the bible appears: "You shall know the Truth and the Truth shall make you free." (John VIII, 32)

I pray that the pages which follow in this book, by the liberty of their appearing, will help to shed light upon what we must do, and do without, if we are to preserve our precious freedom.

Marjorie Wade Fluor

ABOUT JOHN WAYNE

He is known world-wide as "Mr. America"—a man "bigger than life"—the "Duke."

Sure, he is one of the all time great film stars, but that is only his trade. Beneath lies a thoughtful man of rare integrity and candor, deeply concerned about the lack of public resistance to the swollen and reckless federal bureaucracy, spawned by an irresponsible Congress, and spending his beloved America into bankruptcy. He foresees the inevitable consequence thereof—the loss of individual freedoms as the insatiable appetite for power and control over every aspect of our lives continues its cancerous growth in Washington.

He is horrified over the continuing inflation that haunts our nation, brought on by bigger and bigger deficit spending and, in his many public appearances, always without pay, he continues to fight the good fight for us all.

President Jimmy Carter has proclaimed: "John Wayne is a great national asset."*

Carry on Duke! You are a true patriot and America loves you!

*During telephone call to son Michael Wayne at Massachusetts General Hospital.

MESSAGES FOR AMERICA

By JOHN WAYNE

The editorials which appear throughout this book have been produced by the Warner & Swasey Company, Cleveland, Ohio, over the last 40 years. They have proven to be uncannily prophetic. They point the way back to sanity in government and represent the finest collection of hard, Yankee common sense and pure Americana that, in my belief, have ever been assembled.

They lay bare the cold fact that government has no wealth, and when a politician promises to give you something for nothing, he must first confiscate that wealth from you—either by direct taxes, or by the cruelly indirect tax of inflation.

They are terse, exciting and inspiring. They should quicken the heart beat of every patriotic American who ponders them: Widely read, and heeded, they can "turn on" America and "tune out" the dangerous apostles of government providence for all.

They can lead to a resurgence of the spirit of 1776 when our founding fathers laid down the ground rules for structuring the strongest, the richest, the most charitable country on earth, and the staunch defender of freedom loving people everywhere.

Read on, and proudly hail the heritage we must never forsake!

John Wayne

Men are qualified for civil liberties in exact proportion to their disposition to put moral chains upon their own appetites.

— Edmund Burke

"Dreams of a good society have no chance of fulfillment unless our government conducts its financial affairs responsibly. This condition is essential to bringing an end to the inflation that has been raising havoc with our economic institutions; it is essential also to the preservation of our democratic system."

—ARTHUR F. BURNS
Chairman, Federal Reserve

THE COMING BREAKPOINT

A shocking disclosure of invisible, unelected and uncontrolled government, squandering the taxes and violating the freedoms of the American people.

By U.S. SENATOR BARRY GOLDWATER

ABOUT BARRY GOLDWATER

At a time when the hallmark of politicians seems to be to "play the game" in whatever way is expedient to advance self interest, or get re-elected, Senator Barry Goldwater is a shining contradiction.

If one were to describe the attributes which made him so, in the forefront would be *integrity*, *courage* and *candor* and the compulsion t always "tell it like it is." These are words not to be bandied about nor promiscuously applie to public figures because even the most exalted do not always bring clean hands to the furtherance of their ambitions. They are words that can be applied to Barry Goldwater because the conduct of his life has earned ther

Few men in public office have had his rare quality of attracting total "believability" in their sincerity and truthfulness. Dwight D. Eisenhower comes to mind as one other who had it.

A recent Gallup Poll of the American people revealed that, for them, he remains one of the world's ten most admired men. He has been described in the New York Times as one of the few political heros left in the United States.

In the 1964 election campaign he showed his countrymen that, if the choice had to be made he would rather be right than president. He still believes that Americans long for straight answers from their elected officials.

Barry Goldwater has never traveled the politicians' traditional road of "going along" with public acquiescence of their government' directions when he knew them to be wrong. That is why his latest book, THE COMING BREAKPOINT is *must* reading for every citizen who cares about his future, or that of his family and his country.

Because he has held a "front row seat" in government for over a quarter of a century, and because he always "tells it like it is," the reader who wants to get at the truth about the frightening perils confronting his freedom, an that of the nation, will find it to be a welcome revelation.

He will then, hopefully, invoke his duty as a citizen to use his voting franchise to start reversing the tide of total dictatorship from Washington before it is too late.

The book has been condensed for quick and provocative reading in the 46 pages which follow.

THE RIGHT TO TAKE ACTION AGAINST
THE COMING BREAKPOINT *

By U.S. SENATOR BARRY M. GOLDWATER

TELLING IT LIKE IT IS

The Road to Ruin

I hope I can convey to the reader the deep concern I feel about the direction in which our country has been heading for too long a time.

In stark terms, our economic survival is being jeopardized, and the question facing us is whether the working population of America can indefinitely carry an ever-increasing burden of government spending to support the nonworking segment of our society.

If we continue on our present course, with annual enlargements of the welfare state, we will inevitably reach a breakpoint —a place in time where the taxpayer's ability to withstand the loan of unlimited government largesse finally gives way. We are rushing toward the breakpoint at blinding speed. If we reach it before effective stop measures are adopted, we could see our Republic collapse and our democracy smother to death under a mountain of government debt, regulation, and red tape.

Who Sounds the Warning?

The frightening thing about the whole situation is the realization of how few responsible people there are, in or out of government, who actually know what is happening. Occasionally, a voice is raised in alarm, but it is either ignored or forgotten in a matter of hours. The most concerned are those who have had a close look at the overall picture of government operations. For example, former Secretary of the Department of Health, Education and Welfare Caspar Weinberger has warned that the nation's growing welfare system, all by itself, threatens the country with bankruptcy. And Roy L. Ash, former director of the Federal Office of Management and Budget, said in an article in *The Wall Street Journal,* "I believe we stand at a watershed point right now on decisions that could be central in determining the

Government Simplification Department

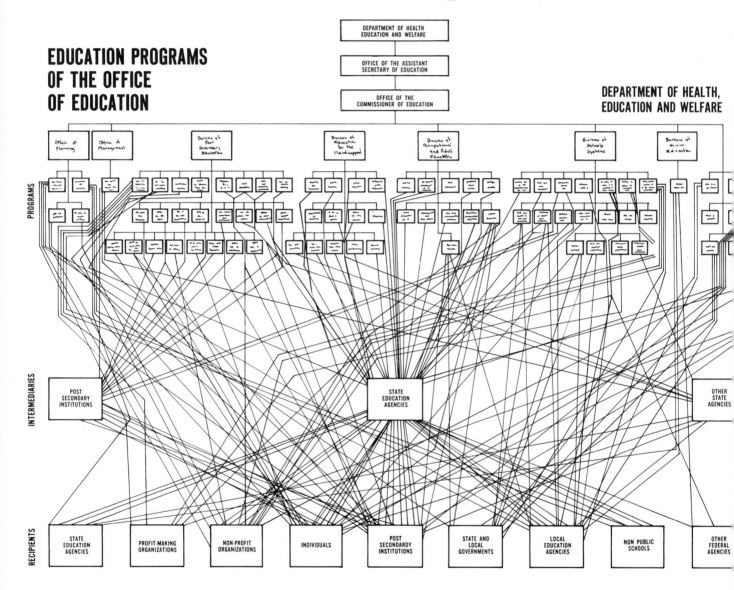

**EDUCATION PROGRAMS
OF THE OFFICE
OF EDUCATION**

DEPARTMENT OF HEALTH
EDUCATION AND WELFARE

OFFICE OF THE ASSISTANT
SECRETARY OF EDUCATION

OFFICE OF THE
COMMISSIONER OF EDUCATION

**DEPARTMENT OF HEALTH,
EDUCATION AND WELFARE**

U.S. OFFICIAL FLOW CHART OF THE OFFICE OF EDUCATION
SHOWN BY HOWARD K. SMITH ABC-TV NEWS PROGRAM FEBRUARY 15 , 1977.

With following comment:

"Government structure is even farther beyond the citizen's comprehension. This maze of boxes and black lines is the flow-chart of the Office of Education in the Department of HEW. No wonder the officials themselves have often had to call in computer experts to tell them what their duties and powers are . . . the laws we must obey have grown far too numerous and thorny . . . the citizen cannot hope to know, on his own, what the law is."

kind of social and political system we will have, not just in our children's time but in our own time."

It is against the backdrop of the coming breakpoint that one of the most fundamental issues in the entire history of America has taken shape and is ready for debate: the tremendous concentration of power in the hands of government bureaucrats and the abuse of that power in the handling of the people's affairs.

I sense an air of finality about the power structure's effort which compels me—reluctantly—to confess that recent events have made me wonder, for the very first time, whether we are equal to making our system of government meet and overcome the challenges and tasks that lie ahead. If we are not, then we may be witnessing the "last hurrah" of the American system of government based on ordered justice.

I desperately wish I could sound an optimistic note. But the fact of the matter is that any political currency I have with the American people stems from my habitual candor. My practice in public has always been to "tell it like it is." Call it a trademark, if you will, but I do believe this trait, which is characteristic of almost a way of life in Arizona and other parts of the Far West, is the "extra something" which many times has set me somewhat apart from my colleagues in the Congress.

Having made this clear, I believe it is time to tell the American people that economically, morally, materially, and otherwise, our country is in the kind of deep trouble that has been known to touch off worldwide depressions and wars. And what bothers me most is that while the trouble was building up, nobody seemed to have the slightest idea of what to do about it, when to do it, or where to find the courage to do it. Some sound suggestions were made but the Congress seemed to lack the fortitude to act upon them.

The Courage To Act

For almost two decades, I, along with other conservatives, have been warning the United States that it was following the same course every other nation had taken before it collapsed and became just another tombstone along the road of history. Now that the day of reckoning is actually bearing down on us, I dearly wish I could forget all that is happening and sit out the rest of my years on my beloved hill in Arizona.

But I cannot do that. If ever there was a time for the advocates of economy and constitutional government to do what they can to help avert total disaster, this is it. And if ever there was a time for publicly identifying the pockets of power in the bureaucracy, with their accompanying threat to individual freedom, this is it. The economic situation facing the United States is just short of desperate and one of the things the nation needs most is the help and advice of those in Congress and in government who have spent years fighting for balanced budgets, reduced government spending, payments on the national debt, and a tough-minded policy toward those sweet-sounding but expensive programs of social engineering. We also need the help of like-minded people in electing Congresses with the courage to act in the interests of all Americans.

Americans Can "Take It"

Most federal officials, and a great many congressmen and senators, know the true state of affairs and have known it for some time, but most of them appear afflicted with a strange disease that manifests itself in a conviction that the American people should not know the truth or that "it can't happen here."

Well, Americans have the guts to take the bad news and the intelligence to do what is necessary to reverse our downward trend. This has been proven time and time again throughout the two-hundred-year history of this country, yet everyone, especially those in the new Administration, tiptoes around as though the opposite were true. But I repeat, the American public can take it—the trouble is that for months on end nobody has told them just what they will have to take.

Yes, I know all the arguments against this kind of painful forthrightness. But none of them offer any justification for withholding the truth from American citizens, especially since to do so, for all my critics know, could actually be a life-and-death matter.

Can Our System Really Work?

America is truly a contrivance of honor and it holds together only so long as the cement adheres. That cement has weakened over the past four decades through the ascendancy of an executive bureaucratic organization so extensive that no one person can actually define its limits in precise terms. And here we encounter the seeds of government disaster and collapse—the kind that wrecked ancient Rome and every other civilization that allowed a sociopolitical monster called the welfare state to exist.

Our Capitol dome doesn't remind us of anything in particular but, rather, of the whole wonderful concept of our government. However, during the past several years we have been learning of some very distasteful, dishonest, unethical, and immoral practices that have gone on in high places in the nation's capitol. Now maybe it is time to take a peek under the great dome where the two Houses of Congress sit, debate, and make decisions to see how power is used and/or abused there and to get a better understanding of procedures such as the seniority system of committee assignments that do not always provide the best leadership or the best legislation.

In the course of what follows, I shall also define the power wielded by the enormous federal bureaucracy, by the Congress through its committee chairmen, by the labor unions, the regulatory agencies,the intellectuals, the "do-gooders," the news media, the educators, and the civil libertarians.

Of course, not the least of these to be discussed will be the bureaucracy, and since nothing like it has ever before existed in the history of the world, this won't be easy. But we can consider matters such as where the enormous grants of power to the executive came from, when they came, and why. We can try to show how the system works. For example, the vast authority of independent agencies to issue regulations which carry the force of law.

The power of Congress means a lot more than the mere statement that it exists. I believe the American people will be astounded to know about the authority wielded by committee chairmen as well as their staffs. But know it they shall, regardless of what kind of reaction the disclosure generates.

In short, we have too many convenient rugs in the federal establishment under which the bureaucrats can brush their waste, inefficiency, and corruption. It's time to roll back the rugs to see what they've been concealing.

The End of Muddling Through

An argument I hear from the "professional spenders" on Capitol Hill is that "we" (meaning the United States and all its citizens) always "muddle through" no matter how serious the problem. This has happened in America in the past. And it has happened in other countries, at least for a considerable period of time. "Muddling through" worked during the plush, irresponsible years of bread and circuses in ancient Rome; it worked in Austria in the 1920's, when that country was building a huge welfare state. But in both Rome and Austria there came a day which could not be muddled through, and as a result, their economies and their governments collapsed under the weight of their own spending and promises. Therefore our ability to muddle through difficult periods in our past does not necessarily mean that we are sure to muddle through the problems facing us today. I wish it did.

I believe the time has come to tell the American people exactly when and where we went wrong, thus creating the political power crisis that faces the United States today. We must all be in full possession of the facts if we are ever to be able to answer the question: Is man—as man is now constituted—able to govern himself successfully over an extended period of time?

A CONTRIVANCE OF HONOR

The Motivating Spirit

Britain's Edmund Burke once defined the government of the United States as a "contrivance of human wisdom to supply the needs of human beings." Needless to say, I believe the plans laid out by the Founding Fathers for our government were all of that—and something more. I believe our forefathers used as much human wisdom as any men had ever put into a project of this kind—the building of a charter for the governing of a people—and in so doing provided us with protection of our God-given freedoms such as no people before have ever enjoyed.

But I honestly believe that these men were motivated by something beyond wisdom that they incorporated in those historic words which we call the U.S. Constitution. Call it what you will, I like the word "spirit" and I believe that spirit can best be exemplified today by the honor which men sworn to uphold the Constitution bring to their task. Trouble enters when such men disregard honor and abuse the powers given them.

Study the Past

One of the most dangerous practices I have run into since coming to Washington as a senator has been that of intelligent, highly educated men and women absolutely refusing to heed the lessons of history. Every day I drive past the National Archives Building and each time I automatically read the words inscribed on either side of that building's entrance: "What is past is prologue—study the past." I often think of this inscription as I sit in the Senate and listen to debate by men who I know have as much knowledge of history as I have, and I wonder why they cannot understand that everything we are doing was done previously at some point in the history of mankind. And always with the same results—some good; some bad.

I wonder why these members of Congress overlook the vital fact that nations and governments and cultures and civilizations have fallen when power was allowed to gather in the hands of a few, and continue to vote more and more power into the hands of the select few who run the many bureaus of our government. From the days of Hammurabi, this has been a sure road to ruin. These bureaus and agencies formed because Congresses in the past, refusing to take the responsibility for solving problems, merely turned them over to an assemblage of people who, while perfectly honorable and devoted to America, were unaware that a concentration of power has always marked the destruction of the people's efforts to govern themselves.

Indeed, what is past is prologue. If only the members of Congress would remember this fact and stop trying to deceive themselves and their constituents into believing that everything is new and that old problems can be solved by devices which have always failed!

The Fundamental Conviction

It should be kept in mind that the framers of the Constitution and the Declaration of Independence went back to the beginning to find their building materials. They reached a conviction that the simple fact of man's birth—the mere entrance of an individual into the human race—of and by itself, marked that individual as the most important of God's earthly creations. And having decided this, our forefathers agreed that all men were born equal and thereby endowed with certain God-given, not man-given, rights automatically entitling them to a certain dignity and respect which they could carry into their meetings and dealings with other human beings. They further agreed that each human being should be free to build his own life without interference from other individuals or groups of individuals.

It was Jefferson who predicted future happiness for Americans if, as he put it, "we can prevent the government from wasting the labors of the people under the pretense of taking care of them."

Viewed against the backdrop of the welfare state (circa 1978), these words have a special and a frightening meaning for American citizens. They involve a matter of such enormous importance that it will be dealt with in considerable length later on. For the moment, it is sufficient to note that Jefferson was an expert on the historical reasons for the demise of past governments and past civilizations. Yet, despite his expertise in the history of government failures, he had great faith in the durability and staying power of the U.S. Constitution.

The Great Experiment

It should be understood and underscored that we are not speaking here of just any old piece of paper or parchment; rather we are speaking of—and I hope paying tribute to—a document that symbolizes the greatest experiment ever devised to serve the largest number of our people and to afford each and every individual the opportunity to make the most of the gifts and talents with which he was endowed by his Creator. To me that document has always represented the world's most determined governmental attempt to treat all the people of a country fairly, as well as man's best effort to construct a system of equity and justice, one that sees government solely in the role of an agency designed to extend help to the people when it is most sorely needed. Government's role under such a system should be to render service to, not exact service from, those who pay for it and live by its precepts. Its primary responsibility should be to use as little power as possible to get a job done for the taxpayers, and even that power should be diffused as much and as quickly as possible to prevent the seeds of totalitarianism from growing and catching hold in a way that eventually leads to dictatorship.

The Constitution, as structured, contains safeguards against the usurpation of state powers by the federal government. But the history of how we have honored that provision—letting it slowly erode and ignoring it altogether in the last few years—is too well known to need repeating.

Can Ends Justify Means?

We have always done these things for a good cause. We have abandoned altogether any constitutional notion of states' rights for such worthy goals as equality of education. We have entrusted to the executive branch extraordinary powers for the purpose of enhancing minority rights or getting through an energy crisis or for the sake of peace, though more recently, when we take them away, we refer to them as war powers. We have done these things willingly and with good intent. But while my conservatism informs me that men are the masters of events, my experience teaches me that men are also influenced by the events and trends that occur around them.

By the 1960's, after we in Congress had been circumventing the laws for years, our constituents, in significant numbers, began to emulate us. They sat in, burned draft cards, fled the draft —always, as we had, for a "good cause"—peace, civil rights, or whatever. By the early seventies there were new demonstrations, new ways to dishonor the laws. This time, those involved were teachers, truckers, politicians. Though they struck illegally or demonstrated or acted illegally, they, too, did it for a "higher law" or higher pay, or a president's re-election.

There are some who would say this trend is inevitable. I would say only that there is precious little to prevent it, save the mortar which is there to hold our laws and our people together, in a contrivance of honor.

THE POWER BUILDUP

Fear Founded in History

When the Founding Fathers sat down two hundred years ago to write a new contract of government for the United States, their greatest fear was that a centralized accumulation of power would ultimately destroy their best efforts.

They had learned to fear the arrogance of power. In Europe, where most of them had come from, they had seen authority run rampant over the inherent rights of the people. Their knowledge of history had taught them that one civilization after another had succumbed when government power became concentrated in one place or in one person, so they were determined to formulate a charter of government that would withstand such a dangerous threat. They labored long and hard to build a system of ordered justice, and erected checks and balances to keep it on balance.

Yet today America's federal establishment has become an overbearing, arrogant concentration of raw power. It is the largest business in existence, with a payroll so enormous it takes a committee of the Senate almost full time just to keep track of it; the paperwork alone costs the taxpayers billions of dollars a year.

Everywhere you look in the nation's capitol there is evidence of the gargantuan federal power. Everywhere you look you see a government bureaucracy so large that nobody ever tries to measure its dimensions any more. And everywhere there is power—federal power—wielded by a group of men and women not elected or even heard of by the public. Thus, bureaucrats who never ran for office, who never received a single vote from the electorate, are busy every day pumping American power around our country and the free world, making it felt in nations, states, cities, and towns throughout the entire globe. This power is something which affects and hurts us all.

When our Founding Fathers deliberately set out to construct a government of laws, not men, they attempted to shelter it under a system whereby the three branches of our government—the executive, legislative, and the judiciary—could balance each other out and prevent the lodgment of undue power in any one segment. And the United States of America, working under this novel Constitution, did extremely well for the first 153 years of its existence. It made democracy an international government fad and injected a healthy jolt of idealism and discipline into the affairs of other nations.

The Origins of Power Buildup

Then in 1933, while we were experiencing an economic depression of unusual severity, along came a president who learned the meaning of power and how it could best be used by an executive. What's more, Franklin Delano Roosevelt understood better than most previous presidents where political power in the United States was strongest.

And it was right then that the concentration of power so feared by our founders had its beginning.

That was the period which saw the federal bureaucracy begin to build the greatest governmental superstructure of all times. That was when the enormous power of organized labor got its start, when social engineering became a costly and burgeoning way of life in the U.S. government, when the *ad hoc* authority of regulatory agencies took on the force of law, when a once-powerful Congress meekly turned over its authority to the executive bureaucracy and to the chairmen and staffs of its seniority-blighted committees. When FDR assumed the office of president, the legislative branch literally forced upon him, his cabinet, his bureaus, and his agencies the responsibility for all the nation's problems.

The result is what we have today—a centralized government so big it frightens even the men who built it. Washington, D.C., is a power factory of almost unbelievable proportions. It is fueled by more than $460 billion and more than two million eight hundred thousand jobs.

I must say it is difficult for me to assess the reasons why the American people—blessed as they have been with liberty and the idea that liberty and freedom are gifts from God—have permitted the concentration of power and the restraints it places on individual action. All around us we see evidence of a decline in morality, ethics, and responsibility to our form of government and the freedom and enterprise which it encompasses. Frankly, I do not fear communism nearly so much as I fear this decline, and, even if the desire to do so exists, the lack of any effort to stop it at the executive or congressional levels.

In the early days of the New Deal we heard a lot of talk about a redistribution of the nation's wealth. I believe many politicians went around the country mouthing that phrase without ever realizing what it might mean for this country in the near or distant future. The conclusion I have come to is that what FDR was involved in was a deliberate attempt to change the social order of the United States.

Having lived through those traumatic days, I'm not going to say that our social order did not require changing, neither am I going to say we have accomplished a great deal in moving our society along the road. But I will say that the question that bothers me most in the whole general field of social endeavor wasn't even considered forty, thirty, or even twenty years ago. That question is whether a new social order in the United States can be sustained by the efforts of a few industrious citizens. In short, I am plagued with wondering whether the few can provide for the many.

Now, if we say they can, we are saying that the money produced by a decreasing percentage of our population is supporting an increasing percentage of the population. If this could happen to any degree, then where is the breakline? In other words, at what point do we find that the social order can no longer change solely as the result of an expenditure of money? Or, if we admit that the social order has not been changed in geometric proportion, or even in direct proportion to the expenditure of money, when does the whole structure break down?

The following illustrates a source of power that very few of us had recognized until recent years. It was brought into very sharp focus early in President Ford's tenure, when he asked that the 5.5 percent automatic cost-of-living pay increases be held up for several months to bring about savings of $700-million. At the mere suggestion, civil employees in Washington were up in arms. They added their great power to the power of the bureaucrats they represented and, on the day the vote on the increase was to be taken, filled the halls of Congress, the Gallery, and every niche in the Capitol where a congressman or a senator could be found. With all these people looking down their backs, the congressmen, our national lawmakers, turned down the president's very sensible, logical request. Therefore, because of civil-employee and bureaucratic power, the president's effort to slow down automatic pay increases proved futile.

But in a way we can't blame them. They didn't ask for those automatic pay increases. Congressmen, including senators, saw some political sex appeal in this approach and wrote the increases into law. Those who have been the beneficiaries of their largesse are not about to allow the law to be changed.

The Courage to Say "No"

I think the question boils down to this: Do the Congress and the Administration have the courage to say "No" to such built-in destroyers of monetary security, those built-in creators and accelerators of inflation? If the courage to say "No" is not in these places, then we are saying "No" to a continuation of our strength which has historically been our freedom.

In fact, there doesn't seem to be any evidence of the courage it takes to stand up to those forces in this country who are demanding, just as all eventually unsuccessful civilizations have demanded before, that fewer and fewer of the people work harder and harder to support more and more of the people who are not working.

FDR and the Shift of Power

Like all other problems involving government and the people, two considerations are paramount: governmental power and individual freedom. Earlier, I mentioned that the authority of the legislative branch was literally forced on President Franklin Roosevelt in the early days of the 1930's when this nation's people were unhappy, discouraged, and downright fearful of the future. FDR, perhaps more than any other leader the world has ever known, with the possible exception of Winston Churchill, looked and acted like a man who knew the answers, who had all of our problems in hand, and who could lead us out of economic morass of a depression if only we would supply the tools.

The legislative equipment was already his. The people elected huge majorities in Congress to support him and carry out his legislative programs in the quickest possible time. Immediate, devastating, frightening problems, such as the need to halt banking operations, could not await the time Congress required to debate and hassle over them, so the president was moved into taking unprecedented actions. It is unlikely that any man in American history has ever before been given this kind of power over his fellowmen without even asking for it.

The shift of power to the executive branch began in the winter of 1933-34. At first the power bills were "short-term," one of the first measures being the Civil Works Administration to provide "temporary" federal jobs for the nation's unemployed. By 1935, though, President Roosevelt had decided on a more permanent program called the Works Progress Administration.

The Birth of Social Engineering

The arguments FDR and his team of liberal advisors used on behalf of the WPA sound faintly familiar when repeated today. Harry L. Hopkins, then head of the Federal Emergency Relief Administration and a close friend of the president, assured the nation that direct relief—or a dole—maintains life "not at a subsistence level, but at a level of deterioration." He spoke emotionally of the "loss of skill, the loss of work habits, muscle, and resolve," to say nothing of the individual American's loss of his sense of importance to himself and his family—and to society—should the dole become permanent.

In view of what has happened since, perhaps Hopkins' most memorable statement was this: "The most ominous threat which the unemployed can hold over the present structure is that they should as a class be perpetuated, unwillingly unproductive, and held in a straitjacket of idleness."

Hopkins was right, as we now know. For, with the energetic help of social engineers working for the federal bureaucracy, several generations of unemployed have been peopled with the kind of relief recipients he described and who now heavily influence elections. But few government officials or members of Congress thought that this could or would happen at the time, and as a result, the legislation that was to lay the foundation for the welfare state of today zipped through the Congress with huge majorities.

The cornerstone of this legislation was the Social Security Act which FDR began working on in 1933 and which was signed into law on August 14, 1935. In this period New Dealers made much of the argument that, in this area, the United States lagged decades behind the nations of Western Europe in the development of a comprehensive social security program to take care of the nation's aged citizens in their twilight years.

One-time Secretary of Labor Frances Perkins, in her memoirs of the Roosevelt years, described how the program developed gradually from a general idea into specific legislation. She explained that Roosevelt was determined to have a self-maintaining system—one in which all benefits paid out were to be supported by premiums paid in. "But the suffering of those now out of work, or the aged or dependent or sick, for whom no such premium ever could be paid, challenged our immediate attention," Mrs. Perkins wrote.

"We agreed that we must bring in a program for unemployment insurance and one for old-age insurance. Without too much debate we agreed that in addition...we must recommend what we knew was not insurance but a relief program. It must include old-age assistance, assistance for dependent children, assistance for the crippled and handicapped persons and a continuation of emergency assistance to the unemployed then in operation."

This, then, was where the groundwork for the welfare state was actually laid. This was a very crucial period in the history of our nation. It was the time when Uncle Sam moved into social engineering on a broad and very costly scale, and never came out; the time when we were lining up a long series of federal spending deficits that has caused the trouble with which we are now groping. Now the question is: How many nonworkers can the workers support? We have to know where the line of refusal to support runs in our system. Maybe it runs until it becomes impossible for the workers any longer to handle the job. We need to know the breakpoint.

Very few people today realize that it was World War II, not the New Deal program, that got us out of the 1930s' depression.

Hard as it is to believe, this nation went from an unemployment crisis in 1937 to a manpower shortage in 1940. It happened so fast that few even recognized the change. However, one thing did not, and has not, altered, and that is "welfare." The monster which now threatens to devour us continues to demand and expect the government to finance its every need, regardless of the economic situation existing at the moment. The welfare population has become entirely dependent on government services financed by the industry of others.

Before long the Administration will have to conduct a massive investigation along the lines of the Hoover Commission studies to find out just which people are cheating on them, for the world's largest bureaucracy is spawning an ever-increasing number of fraud charges involving federal officials and recipients of government monies. In aggregate the allegations involve billions of dollars; in the welfare system alone, fraud and mismanagement are alleged to run into the hundreds of millions.

Some of the most serious charges have been brought against the federally insured Student Loan Program, administered by the United States Department of Health, Education and Welfare (HEW). Federal and state officials have begun investigating a long list of these, which include collusion on a nationwide level among federal officials and owners of schools that operate for profit, illegal lending practices of participating banks, and deceptive advertising by some of the schools.

The Wall Street Journal quoted the authorities as saying that the loss to the government could run to $500 million or more. HEW officials claim that stupidity, greed, and inertia "were big factors" in the irregularities now under investigation.

The waste and inefficiency of abusive power in our government are not confined to any one bureau or department, but stretch across the whole sprawling mess we call the federal bureaucracy. Later on, I shall try to point out other instances of irregularities, abuses, and needless expenditures. I shall start with the bureaucrats because I honestly feel this group has more to do with running the government than any other group in the country.

In the last few years—actually, in the period that began with our grave concern over pollution and the creation of an Environmental Protection Agency (EPA)—more and more Americans have been finding their lives regulated by decrees from Washington. Almost unnoticed, the stream of regulations and dictates has become a genuine flood. Most of them are written by bureaucrats whom no one sees and no one has ever heard of.

RED TAPE, WASTE, AND BOONDOGGLES

No government can afford to become emotionally involved in its bureaucratic projects. This is why only the citizens who foot the bill will ever be able to do anything about projects such as the following:

— A $57,000 study by the University of Pittsburgh on "Community and National Integration" in the People's Republic of China.

— A $20,000-a-year study of German cockroaches by the National Institutes of Health.

— A $70,000 project to conduct research on the smell of perspiration from Australian aborigines. This is one of sixteen subprojects concerned with the "zoophysiology" in Alaska. The purpose of the subproject—to learn about man's adaption to his environment—involved a comparison of the Alaskan Eskimo with the Australian aborigine and their reactions to climate.

— An $8,700 grant awarded by the National Foundation of the Arts and the Humanities for a study of the history of comic books in the nineteenth century. The focus of the project was on the social and political style of comic-strip presentations.

— A payment of $500 to a writer for a poem only seven letters long. The poem (all of it) is as follows: "lighght." It was written by Aramo Saroyan, son of author William Saroyan, and was selected for the American Anthology.

— A $46,089 grant to the University of California at Los Angeles for a dictionary of witchcraft entitled *American Popular Beliefs and Superstitions*.

Not only is the idea of a dictionary of witchcraft a ridiculous pursuit to be financed with federal dollars, but it constitutes an unwarranted example of government competition with private industry. Certainly if a great demand exists for such a publication, America has an ample number of publishing houses ready, willing, and eager to meet it. There is a $19,200 study inaugurated to figure out why kids fall off their tricycles. Others which absolutely raise the hackles on the taxpayer's neck these days are studies of toads in Central America, ants in Indo-Austria, wild boars in Pakistan, lizards in Yugoslavia, catfish in India, and whistling ducks in Texas.

In all fairness, some of these projects suffer from bureaucratic stupidity in the way they are described. Some, according to the General Accounting Office (GAO), have a sound basis for their existence in the budget. Others, however, are little bits and pieces pulled together by federal bureaucrats in their efforts to build a personal empire before Uncle Sam gets around to discovering that they are not doing much to justify their existence on the federal payroll.

"Spend It or Lose It"

If the senseless nature of many boondoggle projects is inclined to infuriate the American taxpayer, he would really be up in arms if he knew the actual reason behind these awards, grants, and handouts, which is this: The existence of many of these far-out projects is a drive on the part of federal bureaucrats to spend before the end of each fiscal year on June 30 all the money voted them by Congress. Mike Causey, a columnist for the Washington Post, has kept a close eye on this phenomenon for many years. In the June 16, 1975 edition of the paper he wrote his annual column about what he calls the "spend-it-or-lose-it-derby." Here is the way he describes it:

"...With only 14 days left to participate, some agencies are unloading money with the same zeal as shut-ins sent to a summer clearance sale with a fistful of disappearing dollars. July 1 is the start of a new fiscal year, and many federal offices are disposing of leftover money for travel, office furniture, or just about anything else they can think of.

Under the sometimes cockeyed federal budget system, agencies found guilty of not spending all they have by midnight June 30 will be forced to suffer the humiliation of returning it to the Treasury.

Those agencies know, too, that they will have to face the grillling of congressional committees that will demand to know why the agencies asked for more money than was needed. So the simplest way to keep everybody happy and stay out of trouble, some believe, is to buy everything in sight until the money is gone.

An example of the bad came a few years ago. One executive branch agency discovered, to its horror, that pots of money were left over with July 1 staring the agency in the face. Rather than suffer the slings and arrows of hard-eyed Treasury auditors and congressional budget bulldogs, the agency took the easy way out.

It ordered, paid for and had installed—all before the June 30 deadline—a batch of fancy and very, very expensive oak doors for the offices of its bigwigs. Previously, the officials had nice doors on their inner sanctums but not the rich oak slammers which remain to this day the envy of other departments...

The spend-it-or-lose-it system is partly the fault of congressional committees, who provide funds in the name of the taxpayers, and the government's short-range 12-month budgeting cycle..."

The Growing Disgust

Public disgust over this high-handed extravagance is fortunately becoming more and more vocal.

The National Science Foundation, for example, has recently come under strong criticism from Sen. William Proxmire for wasting the taxpayers' money on questionable social science research projects such as:

— A $132,500 University of Minnesota study to determine why people fall in love.

— A $342,000 Michigan State University study on the use of birth control devices by unmarried college students. The study questioned 1,200 students as to when, where, and with whom they had premarital sex.

— A $350,000 study on nonconformity which found that 48 percent of the American people believe in the Devil.

— A study to determine how to integrate hitch-hiking into the transportation system.

While Administration officials preach economy, hundreds of White House employees avail themselves of free picture-framing services that cost the taxpayers $92,000 each year.

While the White House urges Americans to conserve gasoline, eight hundred federal officials are chauffered around the capital in limousines.

The government maintains two plush resorts for the sole use of high federal officials, members of Congress, and civilian VIPs. One is in Virginia's Shenandoah National Park; the other, a lakeside mansion, is in Grand Teton National Park in Wyoming. Walter Cronkite and his family were recent guests at one of these taxpayer-supported resorts.

Rep. Robert Drinan (D-Mass) recently had his entire 1974 voting record printed in the Congressional Record for "informational purposes." The cost for the twenty-two-page record: $5,720. If each member of Congress had his voting record printed in the Record each year using as many pages as Drinan, it would cost the taxpayers over $3 million annually.

The Equal Employment Opportunity Commission had a case backlog of 100,000 complaints and had illegally spent $800,000 before it finally came under fire from Congress, which forced the commission to suspend three high officials for twenty days without pay, and demanded that henceforth the GAO audit the EEOC accounts.

There is a national commission on gambling, set up by a 1970 law. The commission's goal is a 1979 report to determine how widespread gambling really is and what rules the federal government should make concerning it. The commission seeks to conduct surveys to find out how many Americans bet, how much they bet, how many are compulsive gamblers, and so forth.

The House Appropriations Subcommittee on Labor-HEW overwhelmingly rejected a proposed budget recision of $291.7 million in Hill-Burton funds which subsidize the construction of hospitals—even though the director of the Hill-Burton project testified that there is an excess of hospital beds in most areas of the country.

How Much is Too Much?

Why all the ire about government spending on "social programs"? Because by 1980 an estimated 40 percent of the national income will be spent on knowledge-related activities compared with just 25 percent for manufacturing. From Kevin Phillips' book, *Mediacracy:**

—In 1948 the federal government spent $1 billion for research and development; in 1974 it spent $20 billion.

—In 1940 national expenditures for education were $3.2 billion; in 1973 they were $96 billion.

—In 1953 HEW spent about $2 billion; in 1976 it spent $140 billion.

The late Sen. John McClellan (D-Ark.), as chairman of the Senate Appropriations Committee, pointed out that federal outlays for social programs—education, manpower, health, and income maintenance—have more than tripled in the last ten years, from $79 billion to $255 billion.

Recent news that the American people are at long last beginning to take matters into their own hands to curb the excesses and arrogance of the federal power brokers is encouraging. It has long been my belief that the only way we can make any progress against bureaucratic power is by the American people becoming sufficiently aroused to demand change.

*New York, Doubleday, 1975.

WHO RUNS THE GOVERNMENT?

Who actually runs the government?

I can tell you for certain it is not the president of the United States, his cabinet, nor the Congress. It is the army of government bureaucrats in Washington and across the nation who hold the kind of power it takes to complicate the lives of American citizens and destroy the freedoms which the Founding Fathers intended them to have.

The bureaucracy which dominates the federal government today has actually become a problem of man's ability to govern himself in a time of tremendous technological change and population growth. It is so massive that it literally feeds on itself, so intricate that it lends itself to a wide range of abuses, some criminal and deliberate, others unwitting and inept. It is so large that no one in or out of government can accurately define its power and scope, and institutions doing business with it, or attempting to do business with it, are forced to hire trained experts just to show them through the labyrinth made up of hundreds of departments, bureaus, commissions, offices, and agencies.

Every now and then we catch a frightening glimpse of this enormous structure and what it means in terms of accountability and manageability. For example, a young member of the House of Representatives several years ago set out to determine how many assistance programs were maintained by the federal government. It took him two years to find out that there were over 1,300, many of which were unknown to each other, unknown to anyone within the government itself, and unknown to the people they were established to help.

Then we had the spectacle several years ago of the House of Representatives engaging in a tense, prolonged, and emotional battle over the appropriation of funds for rat control in our major cities. After all the shouting had died down, it was discovered that eight programs already existed in various government departments for the purpose of doing the same thing!

The size of the federal bureaucracy—which, like Topsy, just keeps growing year after year despite the unfair and growing burden it places on the taxpayer—is compounding the difficulty and confusion that the average American encounters as he attempts to function in today's society. If this continues, the day will come when not only will business choke to death on government red tape, but the average American wage earner and property holder will suffocate under the centralized power that our founders made such efforts to prevent.

Thwarting the Congress

I've already mentioned the evils inherent in this gargantuan monstrosity, which by its very nature lends itself to every kind of abuse. I've also spoken of how its intricacies play into the hands of people skilled in the manipulation of such matters. Now I want to emphasize how this bureaucracy problem thwarts the work in which we in the Senate and the members of the House are engaged. It should not, but probably would, astound most members of the Senate to find out what actually happens to the intent we write into major legislation when it gets into the hands of the bureaucrats. Much of our purpose in enacting laws has been either contradicted, overruled, diluted, or denied by government regulatory agencies, federal enforcement policies, or by the courts.

For example, take our latest government program, the Environmental Protection Agency, which was instituted in 1970. The bureaucrats in this agency are interested in clean air, pure water, and so on. I wish them the greatest luck in their current and future endeavors, for there can be no doubt that the American people have misused their most precious heritage, nature, and pollution is becoming a problem of monumental proportions. I believe there was a need for the Environmental Protection Agency and the Clean Air Act it was given to enforce. But having been there when the original proposals were debated and voted upon, I can assure you that the people operating EPA are going far beyond the intent of either the Congress or the president in the way they have started to implement their responsibilities.

The EPA-Detroit Scandal

Never was the EPA, with or without the help of Ralph Nader, created to build automobiles. Nonetheless, for years EPA has been around with its "made-in-Washington" blueprints for the carmakers in Detroit. When they met resistance, the regulators finally rested their case on an attempt to force U.S. automakers to adopt "catalytic converters" for all new cars, on EPA's assurance that this was the way to reduce exhaust emissions. Detroit finally got tired of the argument and equipped about 85 percent of the 1975 cars with the controversial converters which, incidentally, raised the price of a car by approximately $320. Skeptics who pointed to flaws in the new device were quickly overridden because of the "heat" from Washington and because EPA officials were far from receptive to criticism of any kind. They insisted that the catalytic converters had to be "standard equipment" on all 1975 automobiles. Detroit went ahead when even their pleas for slowing down the schedule were rejected.

The environmentalists had the power in this instance and they used it all. They overpowered not only the automobile industry, but also independent authorities such as the National Academy of Sciences, which also warned against rushing full speed ahead on the converter program.

But EPA won—and then the fun began. All the problems predicted by the skeptics developed, as well as some problems they hadn't even thought of. It almost seemed as though the converter had been waiting to be installed in a car just to show how much trouble it could really cause.

In all events, the carmakers that met EPA's deadline soon learned that leaded gasoline damages the converter's mechanism. They also learned—and this was the clincher—that the converters emitted sulphate mists, which are potentially more harmful to human health than the exhaust emissions they were supposed to prevent.

Only now, as this is written, have the EPA bureaucrats admitted that they bought a "lemon" when they began promoting the converter as a prime antipollution device. Russell Train, director of the EPA, didn't say it that way (bureaucrats never admit costly errors); rather he announced that EPA was relaxing and revising its emission standards, so the converters wouldn't be needed on 1976 model cars. Not a word was said about the sulfuric acid emissions produced by the converters that made widescale use too dangerous even to contemplate.

There is no way to estimate the cost of this goof-up on the part of the EPA regulators. Some people figure it runs into billions of dollars.

This is one of the latest and perhaps one of the most telling examples of the way Uncle Sam can louse up an entire industry with its Big-Brother-knows-best approach to solving the nation's problems. The EPA's obsession with the installation of catalytic converters should serve as a warning to Congress to act cautiously toward any other such proposed measures that could create even more bureaucratic monstrosities. We have enough economic problems at present. What we don't need is another bureaucracy like the EPA, which has an affinity for stupid decisions that cost the taxpayers hundreds of millions of dollars. Let me say again right here that the Congress has already given away too much power to groups and bureaus that do not know how to use it.

The "Tenuritis" Sickness

This whole business of the intent of Congress being thwarted, nullified, or changed by a group of nameless, faceless bureaucrats has gone on too long and has caused too much trouble. What makes these people believe they know so much more than the men who devise and enact the laws? I'll tell you exactly what it is. These men and women are suffering from "tenuritis," by which I mean they have, because of Civil Service, held the same government jobs for so long that they feel the jobs are part of their own personal ideas.

The obstinacy and stubbornness of bureaus that have been too long controlled by men of all major political persuasions proves to me the truth of Lord Acton's famous aphorism: "Power tends to corrupt; absolute power corrupts absolutely." To my mind the power possessed and exercised by the bureaucrats in Washington represents the most dangerous situation in America. If the wrong man should come along and be elected president, we could see a dictatorship erected almost overnight, and it would stem from the loss of power resulting from Congress' failure to live up to its responsibilities. Because the power held in these bureaucratic agencies is power given to them by the Congress which—and I must tell it like it is—was just too damned lazy to take on the job itself.

But I want to point out right here that this rigid, long-entrenched system, deeply dedicated to its own concept of what is right and what is wrong in the realm of government policy-making, is a denial of the democratic process. We have the will of the people being expressed in the election of new administrations. We have the concern of the people reflected in the elections of new officeholders, new policymakers. But the question is whether the people's will, the people's concern, the people's officially stamped request for a change in direction can ever be completely realized under the present system of bureaucratic management. I do not think that it can be. I do not think that the will of the people and the intent of Congress go deep enough into the places where most of the policies directly affecting the people are made. Given the intricacies of the system, the attitude of those in permanent positions, and the general confusion surrounding any change of command in an enterprise as vast as the federal government, I do not think it is possible for this job to be done with any degree of success.

Change Becomes Impossible

No presidential candidate can honestly promise that he will, if elected, make the changes called for—because he can't do much of anything unless the bureaus say "Yes." And the entrenched bureaucrats resist change. They have little or nothing to gain by reform, revision, or innovation. The career executives in charge of the management level of government have learned through long experience to lean and shift with policy-change suggestions coming down from the top, and so they make the absolute minimum number of concessions or none at all to policy pronouncements by cabinet members and bureau chiefs.

What we are dealing with here is an administrative maze so complex that many newly appointed policymaking officials spend almost their entire term of office trying to find out precisely what their duties, responsibilities, and functions are. The system lends itself to all kinds of abuse but its major drawback is its enormous, unfathomable size. New cabinet members are often criticized for not having a firmer grasp of the problems relating to their agencies. Very seldom do the critics stop to realize that a mere presidential appointment does not make an administrative expert.

This subject is so involved that it would take many hours, even days to do it justice. What I have tried to do here is to detail some of the threatening aspects of the federal bureaucracy and to suggest that it is time to consider new approaches and fresh attitudes in our consideration of how to reduce its power and make it more responsible to the needs of the American people and freedom.

Loss of Congressional Control

Candor compels me, however, to acknowledge that a large—perhaps the largest—part of the responsibility lies with the legislative branch of the government, at least in the initial phase. In fact, in the area of what government experts refer to as "the principle of accountability," the Congress has simply lost control over most of the money expended by the Treasury each year.

And again I stress that this control has been lost to men who were not elected and who are not directly responsible to the people.

They cannot be voted out of office if they make costly mistakes, yet they manage the offices in thousands of government buildings, and buy, sell, lend, and borrow assets; manipulate credit, pools, funds, contracts; oversee obligations, debts, accounts; have the authorization to spend from debt receipts and to fix payments and rates. And so on and so on.

I am fully aware that it is all too easy for those of us who do not have direct responsibility to assign blame and hand out rhetorical prescriptions as to what should be done to improve departmental performances. I know it is a problem which is not going to be corrected overnight. Nor is it one which easily lends itself to any pat solution. I do, however, believe there is great need at the present time for the enlistment of men and women with experience of overall planning techniques. As a class, these are people who not only have imagination and experience in general planning and analysis, but who also are more interested in innovation and problem-solving than in the perpetuation of their jobs or in the impact of their views on the formulation of policy.

A Time for Action

There are many ways in which this enormous bureaucratic problem can be tackled. I personally am not wedded to any particular stratagem or method, but I do believe very strongly that the time is long past when something should have been done and hence no further time should be wasted before conducting an in-depth study of the situation. The resultant recommendations should then be acted upon at once; otherwise the will of the people and the intent of the Constitution will continue to disappear in the giant federal bureaucratic maw.

As things stand now, our democratic form of government, in its most fundamental sense, is in danger. I only hope that what I have said here will underscore the importance of understanding what we are up against and encourage those in positions of responsibility to take some courageous and drastic action to meet it effectively.

FEDERAL WORKERS, THE BUREAUCRACY, AND INDIVIDUAL FREEDOM

People and Paperwork

Almost half the new jobs being created these days are in government—federal, state, and local. The total in 1976 exceeded 14 million and cost the taxpayers an estimated $315 billion for salaries and fringe benefits.

As the hiring rate steadily increases, one question that arises is: How long can the nongovernment workers support Uncle Sam's work force?

The Office of Management and Budget estimates that organizations and individuals have to spend 130-million man-hours a year to cope with the mounting glut of federal forms. American business, of course, takes first prize for the number of government forms it has to fill out; its paperwork, as a consequence, has increased by 50 percent since 1967.

Paperwork, of course, helps out the paper industry and creates new jobs. But it doesn't add to the country's Gross National Product or industrial output. Instead, what too often results is nothing but wasted time and unusable data to be stored in 300,000 bureaucratic buildings.

Shutting Down Uncle Sam?

But the paperwork blizzard is nothing compared to what could happen to this country if all public employees obtain and use the right to strike. Congress has before it right now a measure that would permit federal workers to strike. When you take into consideration public workers at the state and local levels, this would mean that some 14 million public employees would be permitted to leave their jobs any time they felt a grievance. We could, with the kind of labor-controlled Congress we have today, see a nationwide rash of strikes that would cripple transit facilities, hospitals, and schools, or produce, nationwide, a garbage glut such as New York experienced some time back when the sanitation workers in that city decided to strike.

With the increase in power held by the nation's bureaucrats, there is a corresponding increase in the power of a labor leader named Jerry Wurf.

Wurf is the international president of the American Federation of State, County and Municipal Employees (AFL-CIO). He is reported to be one of the most powerful of the nation's labor leaders. His union of government employees is the fastest-growing one in the country and this spells big trouble for the taxpayer and more turmoil in public service for the future.

Most of the people who make up the membership of Wurf's union are unknown to the public at large, but they make decisions or nondecisions that reach into the lives of 215 million Americans.

These petty decision-makers grant, withhold, or revoke broadcasting and TV licenses; levy penalties on cheating taxpayers; tell employers whom they must hire and how much they should pay them. In the opinion of many observers, these bureaucrats are becoming the new bosses of the United States without the public being any the wiser.

Sex Break

People who are aware of the public-employee situation actually wonder whether it has gotten beyond all control. And they might well wonder when it comes to the latest fringe benefit that the federal employee unions are now said to be considering. Since it involves sex—repeat, sex—in a very direct way, labor circles are regarding it as "the offer they couldn't refuse." The benefit was discovered by Joseph Young, a columnist for the Washington Star, who, "in a spirit of helpfulness," called it to the attention of the unions.

Mr. Young acknowledged that the idea—certainly one of the most esoteric and erotic ever to be considered seriously as a legitimate fringe benefit—did not originate with him. He says he got it from reading the Labor Management Relations Service Newsletter, the official publication of the National League of Cities of the United States Conference of Mayors and the National Association of Counties.

The newsletter, knowing that the members of these groups are the officials who have to deal with the public employees' unions, called attention to a report from the Fiji Islands, which dealt with a gold miners' union in Suva and its demand for a fringe benefit known as the "nooners." It seems the miners' union wants, as part of its current contract, a 30-minute mid-day "sex break" for its members.

The union secretary was quoted as saying that the miners believe mid-day is the best time for men and women to engage in sexual relations, and union officials reportedly are arguing that if a man comes home at 5:00 P.M. exhausted and dragged out from a full day's work in the mines, he won't be able adequately to fulfill his sexual obligations to his wife. Accordingly, the union is asking for a half-hour sex break in addition to the normal lunch period.

I doubt if even John L. Lewis or Philip Murray ever heard of a fringe benefit called the "sex break." In all events, it seems to be here and I'll bet it's here to stay.

Congressional Inflation

Some observers are inclined to believe that something can be done in Congress to curb the excess of unionized public employees. Maybe it can, but the trouble is that Congress shows every indication of waffling on the question. What's more, the Congress is playing the same game with the same people by whom it is controlled. Let's take a look at where the Congress stands on the question of bureaucratic expansion.

A close study will reveal that everything in Congress has increased except its performance on behalf of the overburdened public. The budget and staff on Capitol Hill have swelled phenomenally.

For example, in 1954 Congress employed 4,500 people and operated on a budget of $42 million. In 1974 Congress employed 16,000 people and had a budget of $328 million. And let me tell you it takes more than the kind of inflation we've just had to justify a staff increase of 256 percent and a budget increase of 681 percent. Just to accommodate the physical growth of the staff, Congress has overflowed into two more buildings and has contracted for another $34 million office building.

At this rate, by 1984 it will cost $1 billion to operate Congress.

What results from the tremendous increase in congressional personnel is a comparable increase in the number of amendments suggested for major pieces of legislation. Most of the amendments are written by staff members, rather than by the senators themselves; in fact, few members know precisely what is contained in or what might issue from these amendments. Consequently, there is an expanded volume of poor legislation.

Public insight into this expansion is very limited. Although Congress oversees the budget of the entire federal bureaucracy—including the president's own staff—Congress alone, unchecked by any other authority, decides how much to spend on itself. In the same year that Congress passed a liberalized freedom-of-information act designed to give the public greater access to government bureaucracy records, it voted to close to the public the records of the foreign-travel expenses of House members and their staffs.

The Washington Post recently made an investigation into the staffing practices of Congress and had to use its IBM computer to sort out complicated congressional spending reports and so forth, in order to figure out what was going on.

It found widespread abuse of the committee system-members diverting staff hired for committee business to their own personal staffs; holding numerous "field hearings" to gain publicity in their own states; taking winter vacations, and avoiding payment of full travel expenses to places where they have speaking engagements; building presidential campaign organizations through the accumulation of congressional staff; holding hearings on subjects outside the jurisdiction of a committee.

Exceeding Their Authority

Many times, both publicly and privately, I have complained that too much authority—important authority—is left in the hands of congressional staff members who have no right, and in many cases no ability, to exercise it. I'm not saying that every member of a staff—whether the staff is that of an individual Senator, a House member, or a committe—is inefficient. Far from it. Most staffers are extremely able. But this does not alter the fact that they have been given far too much power by members who are too busy or too lazy to exercise it themselves. This is not right. Nor is it, as I pointed out previously, in keeping with the governmental structure envisioned by the Founding Fathers, because these staff members often exercise the power of decision-making on matters affecting millions of Americans, although they were never elected to do so.

Taxes and Choices

The total amount of taxes paid to local, state, and federal governments has risen 781 percent since 1944. Today the government takes more than one-third of every dollar of income generated in the United States. This means that the average person spends three hours of his average working day paying this tax bill—more than he spends for food, clothing, and shelter.

With this huge and growing tax burden, the government is encroaching more and more into areas previously left to personal choice. We ride monopolized and government-regulated city transit, commuter railroads, taxicabs, airlines, buses, and trains. Our raw materials are delivered and our products are shipped by regulated trucks, trains, barges, and pipelines. Our homes are heated by government-regulated gas. We drink government-regulated water. We read by government-regulated light. Our food is inspected by a government agency. The drugs we take are tested, and in some cases prescribed, under government supervision. The government can limit the amount an individual can spend per child on education, how much he can contribute to political candidates whose views he wishes to support.

In the area of private business, the government has something to say about where a business can build, how it must design its buildings, whom it can hire and promote, how much it must pay employees, what standards its products must meet, how it can advertise its products, how much it can sell them for, and with whom the firm can merge.

Governmental Victimizing of Our Children

And now let us look at some examples of the infringements on personal freedom in the area of education.

American education is being quietly transformed—and the last vestiges of community control stripped away—by recent court decisions that communities may no longer support their schools through local property taxes. Starting with the California Supreme Court in 1971, many state courts have ruled that the financing of schools through local property taxes violates the principles of equal education and equal protection, because it results in the wealthy having more money to spend on education than the poor. As a result, states are being forced to institute the financing of schools. Through this system, the state government decides how much each community will be taxed for schools, collects the money, and then redistributes it in such a manner that no school system is better off than any other. The impact of this on individual communities can be devastating, as the following shows:

New Trier, Illinois: This wealthy community has lost the right to tax itself at a higher rate in order to support its superior local school system. The state required New Trier to cut its local school taxes in order to equalize its educational output with the rest of the state. New Trier must now fire thirty-five faculty and staff members, and the school superintendent told *The New York Times* that this would "make the quality of our education decline drastically."

During my first two terms in the Senate of the United States, stretching from 1953 to 1964, I served on the Subcommittee on Education of the Labor and Public Welfare Committee. I constantly resisted, with all the vigor I could muster, federal aid to elementary education. Naturally, I was stamped as a person with archaic views opposed to education. This, of course, was totally untrue, but the accusations militated against my arguments and the damage was done.

The danger I was trying to point out, particularly to the American mother and father whose children were in school, was that with federal money went federal control; but I could not make Americans understand what it was going to do to the educational system of this country. I was so soundly defeated in 1964 that the Congress took part of that defeat as a mandate to give President Lyndon Johnson everything he asked for, and he was asking for federal aid to elementary education. His request was granted, and as a result, control of what our children are taught was taken from our hands. And while in the years to follow 1964 we saw governmental expenditures on elementary education rise, we also saw the quality of education steadily deteriorate.

To put it as bluntly as I can, the American people and their children are being victimized by federal control of tax money spent on elementary education, because our system of education is ailing to such an extent that it may be on the verge of collapse.

THE REGULATORS

"The Bankruptcy Brokers"

On February 1, 1975, a prominent economist, Thomas G. Moore, of Stanford University, charged during an ABC-TV special on the regulation of transportation that the procedures and red tape in the Interstate Commerce Commission (ICC) are costing Americans $10 billion.

Two days earlier another regulatory agency, the Federal Communications Commission (FCC), had destroyed a Midwest communications business by refusing to renew five of its licenses to operate radio stations.

About the same time, the Food and Drug Administration (FDA) was putting the "kiss of death" on two products sold by one of the nation's largest pharmaceutical firms.

Regardless of whether the economist was correct and regardless of how well-founded the agencies' claims against the businesses were, the thing that bothered me about these actions was the federal government's using every conceivable excuse for sticking its nose into the American competitive enterprise system.

Some people, including some of my colleagues in Congress, seem to think I'm joking when I point out that if a close watch is not kept on the "regulators," it is possible that the federal government will regulate the nation out of business. Well, let me tell you it is not a joke, and anyone who thinks otherwise can check the rate of business bankruptcies in recent years and the reasons given for these failures.

Let me give an example of what I mean. A recent survey by the Office of Management and Budget, on the number of reports required of business from just a few federal agencies, shows that in the summer of 1975, 2,178 different ones were demanded, which took American businessmen the equivalent of 35.6-million man-hours to fill out. In late July, 1975, Secretary of Commerce

Frederick B. Dent told me that by that time the number had increased to 3,000.

Let's assume the average hourly wage for all businesses in the United States is $3 (actually it's much higher). In this case, the cost to business for handling the new paperwork projects would run somewhere in the neighborhood of $105.8 billion, with this sum coming out of company profits, *which are ordinarily used to create new jobs.*

Government regulators never seem to get around to recognizing the effect of their actions on the job market and the economic health of the nation. President Ford put the problem in its proper perspective when he estimated that the annual cost to American consumers of unnecessary and wasteful regulatory policies is $2,000 per family. This means the total cost to the public is an estimated $130 billion.

Businesses regulated include just about every line that human beings engage in to make a living. The big one does what has to be done—hires enough accountants and paperwork experts to tackle the job; the little guy puts up a fight, but eventually goes out of business. For failure to comply with federal directives, each risks fines, jail, or both.

The Chaining of Free Enterprise

We seem to have forgotten that the free competitive enterprise system was once regarded as unique in America. Here in this country is where it was allowed to flourish and bloom. Here is where it has had its best chance to succeed—that is, until Uncle Sam began to interfere in it. Now the free enterprise system, this display-stone of democracy, is being whittled down by government regulations which carry the force of law, even though Congress might not have had anything to do with their formulation.

Through the Federal Trade Commission, the government has something to say about what manufacturers can tell the public about their products. The FTC's original purpose was to investigate only anticompetitive business practices; but its powers were expanded in 1938 to include investigation of deceptive advertising and consumer fraud. "Advertising" means any method by which sellers induce customers to buy their product.

The FTC also appears to be going the way of the FDA using "truth in advertising" to require manufacturers to prove the "effectiveness" of their products.

Some examples of FTC decisions on advertising claims:
—It is misleading the consumer to call a fake fur a "fake fur."
—Discounters cannot advertise with the slogan, Buy One, Get One Free.

—A company cannot say its product is "better than" another product; but it can claim its product is the "best."

—A dime store had to label its turquoise rings to make sure the consumer knew they were not real turquoise.

—A toy company was forced to disclose that its toy did not fire real projectiles that exploded.

—First Prize Bobby Pins had to change their name because the FTC said it led consumers to believe they were eligible to enter a contest.

Recently, the FTC proposed to the Federal Communications Commission that broadcasters be forced to provide air time for replies to commercials. This proposal, however, was rejected.

Meanwhile, all other kinds of abuses of power are exercised by the regulatory agencies. For example, only recently it was discovered that a contract officer who helped write a ten-million-dollar computer contract for the Federal Power Commission once worked for the firm that won the contract. This is only a minor irregularity in the system.

Lawmaking by Proxy

What is involved here is an enormous area of law being written by men and women, appointed to their jobs, who may or may not have had sufficient qualifications to recommend the kind of regulations that would best serve the American public. Some of the regulations are far more important than many of the laws passed by the Congress. For example, the Interstate Commerce Commission regulates everything that moves in commercial channels across state lines. The first regulatory agency ever appointed, it was set up before the turn of the century to regulate railroads and establish proper rates for rail carriers. Now, of course, it also includes truckers, airlines, and the like.

The whole system of the commission's rates has become so complicated that one expert tried using a sophisticated computer to simplify the work of figuring them out. He told the American Broadcasting Company that he had spent five years just putting into the computer all the ICC tariffs affecting his company; and the job was not yet finished.

Very recently a new factor was brought into the regulatory picture when it was discovered that the members of the U.S. Civil Service Commission had been making job recommendations for vacancies arising in the federal system. For example, on thirty-five occasions in the past six years, the three members of the Civil Service Commission had recommended job applicants to officials in federal agencies. This, in effect, set up the Civil Service Commission as a small dictatorship that named the men who recommended the regulations under which American business and American consumers were forced to operate.

As the spotlight begins to focus more and more on regulatory agencies, the Civil Service Commission comes in for more charges. For years the commission has been regarded as a little above the ordinary government bureaucracy, since it was initiated to protect the government from the evils of the spoils system, wherein the winning political party practically emptied the government payrolls and filled them with its own people. But that was many years ago and now the Civil Service Commission has actually become part of the bureaucracy over which it was once expected to act as a watchdog.

Subsidies That Hurt Consumers

The regulators, in the beginning, were named to protect the American consumer. They have not only failed miserably in this task, but have succeeded in seeing to it that much of today's regulatory machinery actually shelters the producers from the normal competitive consequences of lassitude and inefficiency.

In all events, the consumer—however he is being abused—is paying through the nose, and paying plenty, in the form of government-sanctioned price-fixing.

Louis Engman, former head of the Federal Trade Commission, has said that the most distressing development is the pervasive and widely accepted dishonesty that envelops the government's approach to regulation. The existing crazy quilt of anti-consumer subsidies embodied in the intricately woven fabric of federal and state statutes and regulations is pernicious.

In most cases we have adopted the least efficient forms of the subsidies which cost the consumer so much to maintain. Their existence is deliberately hidden from the public or else their actual cost is obscured. Even the government has lost track of how much they cost and their responsibilities concerning them.

Every once in a while proposals are put forth to provide direct cash subsidies in lieu of the patchwork of regulatory subsidies that now blanket our economy. Each time, however, opponents rise indignantly to object that hard-working individuals and hard-working businesses don't want handouts. Like it or not, that is exactly what we're giving them now, whether it's called a cash subsidy or a regulation that does the same job.

Maybe our businesses don't want handouts. If they don't I've wasted one hell of a lot of time listening to arguments in the Senate about how necessary it was to bail the Penn Central and Lockheed out of their monetary troubles.

Actually, I do believe there is an argument that can be used to end protests against Engman's claim that our airlines, truckers, railroads, electronic media, and much more of the business life of the nation are on the dole. It is this: We get all steamed up about wasteful and fraud-ridden welfare projects, and we cer-

56

tainly should, for if something isn't done in that area the hand-outs will eat us up. But I would be something less than honest if I didn't point out that, by comparison, our complex system of hidden regulatory subsidies make the welfare frauds look pretty much like petty larcenies.

Protection—at What Price?

The actions of the Food and Drug Administration offer another dramatic example of how the federal government's regulators interfere with the free operation of the supply-and-demand concepts of the American enterprise system. Every time the FDA labels a food element or a drug "dangerous" to the public health, it plays havoc with some segment of the private enterprise system. Because of this, one of the favorite jokes in the Department of Health, Education and Welfare is that Uncle Sam is the regulator who wants to prohibit the sale of cyclamates because they might prove harmful to public health and legalize marijuana because it might not be harmful to the public health.

Among the other new regulators is the Consumer Products Safety Commission. CPSC has jurisdiction over more than 10,000 products and processes, and possesses the authority to set mandatory safety standards to ban or recall products from the marketplace without a court hearing, to require product warnings by manufacturers, to order rebates to consumers, and even to send offending executives to jail.

Rep. Jamie Whitten, chairman of the House Appropriations Subcommittee on Consumer Protection, was astounded upon learning of the power held by the relatively new CPSC. In a recent hearing he told the chairman of the consumer's group:

"You've got so much power here it's unbelievable...You've got the power of life or death over whether consumers are to have anything to consume."

There is little likelihood that the CPSC would use the full extent of its power—but the mere fact that it exists is awesome. And current plans for the new agency are far from reassuring. Professor Weidenbaum, for example, claims the CPSC is planning to declare the average residence an "unsafe product" and thus bring the entire home under the agency's jurisdiction.

Chairman Richard O. Simpson of CPSC—at least in his public statements—obviously isn't reaching for better business-government relations. Take this assertion, for instance:

"If a company violates our statute, we will not concern ourselves with its middle-level executives; we will put the chief executive in jail. Once we put a top executive behind bars, I am sure that we will get a much higher degree of compliance from other companies."

The Risks of Over-Regulation

There can be no doubt that officials connected with this new and little-known agency are part of the most powerful independent regulatory agency ever created. And there is little doubt that the tremendous increase in demand for information from the federal government stems from this agency. In its first major proposed rule in August, 1973, the CPSC called upon every manufacturer, distributor, or retailer—upon learning that a product it sold had a risk of injury—to provide the commission with a staggering amount of data. Among other things asked for were: the number of products which present a hazard or semihazard; the number of units of each product in the hands of consumers; specific dates when faulty units were manufactured and distributed and an accounting of when and where such products (and the number units of each) were distributed; the model and serial numbers affected; a list of names and addresses of every distributor, retailer, and producer of the product, if known; a description of the effort that has been made to notify consumers of the defects; and details of corrective tests, quality controls, and engineering changes that were made or contemplated.

In addition, the commission shifts to the manufacturer the full burden of determining and remedying potential product defects, while in the background there is the ever-present threat of criminal sanctions should the commission disagree with the company's decision.

There obviously has been no effort to figure out what the effect might be upon the targets of the agency's actions. For example, the commission has indicated that it ultimately may require manufacturers to keep records of all the product complaints they receive and to make them available to the commission upon request.

There probably has never been a regulatory agency established in the federal government which practiced more high-handedness from the very beginning than the CPSC. One of its first cases, in which the agency revealed an excess of bureaucratic zeal or just plain bad judgement, involved the ordering of formal hearings to determine if four million electric frying pans were hazardous.

The fascinating aspect of this case is that out of these four million frying pans, not a single injury had been reported to the commission. Murray Weidenbaum, in reporting on the CPSC's action, stated: "It is no exaggeration to suggest that the commission—unwittingly, of course—may turn out to be the most anti-consumer organization of all time."

Nobody could overlook the Occupational Safety and Health Administration because it is that part of the federal government which makes sure that the cuspidors are cleaned daily in the federal establishments.

In the new period of U.S. regulation, the OSHA comes in for a great deal of attention. It is one of those agencies whose objectives are so worthy that anyone who questions them runs the risk of being called a hard-hearted partisan completely lacking in human compassion. After all, who isn't in favor of improving work environments in which 14,000 Americans were killed in 1975 in job-related accidents?

Even so, the worth of its objective doesn't stop OSHA from ridiculous conduct, such as the promulgation of stupid rules. Even the Federation of American Scientists was moved in 1973 to issue a critical description of the way OSHA operated. It made the following statement:

"Regulations are voluminous and complex; the language is convoluted beyond recognition except by a scientist or lawyer. Worse yet, there is no provision for a penalty-free consultation with an Occupational Safety and Health Administration inspector...The Occupational Safety and Health Act, in short, has created at least as many problems as it was designed to solve."

The agency has gone overboard on the subject of rules and regulations. Some are so long and tedious that the agency's own representatives aren't always familiar with them. As a case in point, when Professor Weidenbaum sent a research assistant to check on an order relating to spittoons, he was assured by the area representative that no such provision existed. But the OSHA regulations published in the Federal Register contain the following statement: "Cuspidors are considered undesirable but, if used, they shall be of such construction that they are cleanable. They will be cleaned at least daily when in use (Title 29, Section 1910, (A) (Z) (ii))."

As minor as this incident is, it nonetheless bothers me because it points up the ease with which federal officials deny, lie, or brush off embarrassing questions from the people who pay their salaries and who worry about others who do the same. What's more, it strikes me that if federal officials can fabricate untrue stories about something as foolish as cuspidors, there is no telling what they could do about more important items owned by the federal government.

Regardless, the toughest criticism of OSHA has not come from business or labor, but from the federal government itself. One of its toughest critics is Chairman Robert D. Moran of the Occupational Safety and Health Review Commission. This is an independent agency created to hear appeals from rulings by OSHA inspectors.

Rules Which Fail to Protect

Moran claims too many standards are (to paraphrase Winston Churchill) riddles, wrapped in mysteries, inside enigmas. They don't give the employer even a nebulous suggestion of what he should do to protect his employees from whatever it is (also left unexplained) which represents a hazard to their safety and health.

After citing one vague and general standard, Moran declared:

"I submit that there isn't a person on earth who can be certain he is in full compliance with the requirements of this standard at any particular point of time."

So far as small business is concerned, interpretation of OSHA's standard is the big problem. Since small businessmen are unable to employ experts to explain bureaucratic regulations, they usually go to the government for help. When they go to OSHA, however, they get material they can't understand or material they don't need. One document suggested by the OSHA guide contains 455 pages of fine print, including algebraic and trigonometric equations. But if someone skips that part of the instruction, he can make the discovery elsewhere in the guide that a ladder is "an appliance usually consisting of two side rails joined at regular intervals by cross pieces called steps, rungs, cleats, on which a person may step in ascending or descending."

And if the person is interested in the hazards that may be related to his departure from a building, he can learn all about the word "exit." The guide tells him that "exit" is "that portion of a means of egress which is separated from all other spaces of the building or structure by construction or equipment as required in this subpart to provide a protected way of travel to the exit discharge. A means of egress is a continuous or unobstructed way of exit travel from any point in a building or structure to a public way and consists of three separate and distinct parts: the way of exit access, the exit, and the way of exit discharge. A means of egress comprises the vertical and horizontal ways of travel and shall include intervening room spaces, doorways, hallways, corridors, passageways, balconies, ramps, stairs, enclosures, lobbies, escalators, horizontal exits, and courts and yards."

The trouble with OSHA regulations, according to Moran, is that many of them are so lacking in uniformity that the agency workers themselves can't tell anyone how to comply with them, for they are not in a position to know if and when regulations have been violated.

Among other things wrong with the Occupations Safety and Health Act is that no provision is made for "courtesy inspections." In other words, a company invites the OSHA inspectors to look at its operations at its own peril. Instead of receiving information on what the government wants, such invitations can easily result in instant citations for some infraction of OSHA rules and regulations. One would think the government would welcome voluntary requests from business firms seeking to know if their facilities measure up to federal standards. This doesn't seem to be the case, however.

So all of this brings us back to Lord Acton's observation that "power tends to corrupt and absolute power corrupts absolutely." I'd still like to find an exception to his maxim, but my despair of ever doing so grows deeper the longer I am in public service. Instead, I'm inclined to believe that a proper and well thought-out delegation of authority holds the answer we're looking for.

LABOR'S CLOUT IN GOVERNMENT

Creating A "Labor Congress"

Not all the power in Washington is wielded by Congress, the regulators, the bureaucrats, and staff experts. The heaviest clout ever held by a lobby for special interests in the United States is that belonging to organized labor today.

A recent book by Douglas Caddy gives a pretty good picture of what I mean. The book, entitled *The $100 Million Payoff: How Big Labor Buys Its Democrats,** flatly labels the labor union operation in recent elections as "illegal" in a way that forms an ample basis for prosecution.

Caddy pulls no punches when discussing his book. In an interview for the newspaper *Human Events* on August 10, 1974, he charged that labor bosses claim they controlled 57 out of 100 members of the U.S. Senate and 230 of the 435 members of the House of Representatives. This gives the United States a "labor Congress" that, according to Mr. Caddy, does not satisfy President George Meany of the AFL-CIO. Meany wants a "veto-proof Congress," which means a Congress in which labor controls two-thirds of the members of both Houses.

Labor's enormous power in Washington disturbs me, but not as much as the way that power was obtained: It was purchased with funds from the fat union treasuries controlled by the labor bosses, who many times do not reflect the desires of the union rank-and-file members who own the money.

*New Rochelle, N.Y.: Arlington House, 1974.

During the Watergate scandal, powerful segments of the news media created the impression that the only campaign abuses occurring in 1972 had been those of business corporations and the Republicans. I submit that my party has no monopoly on campaign irregularities. As a matter of fact, when I think back over the days of bosses like Pendergast, Hague, and others, I wonder if the Democrats didn't actually "write the book" on campaign abuses during the past fifty or sixty years.

Late in its investigation, the Senate Watergate Committee announced it was going to look into the political activities of top union officials. The release of this statement came as a complete surprise to all the union critics in Washington and throughout the country. For example, Reed Larson, executive vice-president of the National Right to Work Committee, expressed the opinion that if the committee went about such an investigation seriously, "the whole shape of politics in America would suddenly change."

But if reform elements were basing their hopes on the Watergate Investigating Committee, they, as the Brooklyn expression goes, "shoulda stood in bed." The Ervin Committee, so far as we can find out, talked to a few people, sent out some questionnaires, and then dropped the whole investigation of labor contributors. Thus the casual observer is left with the impression that this area of politics contained no irregularity worth investigating.

There is nothing especially new about big labor contributions to influential congressmen. For nearly forty years—ever since the enactment of the Wagner Labor Act under FDR—labor unions have enjoyed a special type of privilege and immunity at the hands of the legislators. And I am one of the first to say that when the Wagner Act was passed way back in the thirties, it was long overdue, for American corporations had gone overboard in their unfair treatment of the American workingman. But now the pendulum has swung far in the other direction—much too far for the good of the free enterprise system and for the good of the country.

A Balance: Business, Government, Labor

There really is such a thing as too much power in certain instances. Nonetheless, I am more interested in unused power where the federal government and labor unions are concerned. I say this in the wholehearted belief that labor unions serve an important purpose when kept within legal and reasonable bounds. Some of my friends will no doubt be surprised to read that I am in favor of labor unions, that I believe they perform an important function, and that I support their right to strike. It is my considered opinion that the strike is an expression of freedom on the part of the worker that must be protected. At the same time, I am opposed to compulsory arbitration because I believe that is a denial of freedom. And I am opposed to the growing demand for legislation for compulsory unionism at all levels of government.

What we need, and what I have urged on the Congress for at least fifteen years, is a national labor policy which would treat all segments of our society—especially big business, big government, and big labor—with an evenhandedness not previously exercised.

Contrary to what many of my critics say, I have no desire to see America's labor unions abolished. Nor do I believe it would serve any useful purpose to take from the unions the gains they have made over the years against formidable odds. No, what I'm talking about here is a kind of balance among labor, business, and government that could benefit every single American.

But, believe me, this balance can't be achieved if liberals continue to give labor unions the advantage over all other economic groups. Granted, back in the thirties the labor unions needed help. Well, they got it—and they've been getting it ever since. They have now amassed enormous power in the federal government but they want still more. They want privileges, sanctions, and immunities that are enjoyed by no other segment of the economy.

Labor's "Unfair Competition"

Just to give the reader an example—the unions completely ignore the Federal Corrupt Practices Act which has been on the books since 1947 and under which corporations are prosecuted for making political contributions. In addition, the unions are not liable to the nation's antitrust and monopoly laws, although they apply to all business corporations.

And, of course, the unions continue to use the sometimes-more-valuable-than-cash device of in-kind contributions to whichever candidates they think will vote for labor's objectives. The Republicans, on the other hand, must actually beg their partisans for manpower, equipment, and assistance (such as doorbell ringers, large mailings, telephone blitzes, transportation to the polls, and baby-sitting services) for some of the most difficult tasks to be filled during a campaign and when election day rolls around. The Democrats get all these services free of charge from unions who pay the salaries of the people they send to help their candidates; therefore the helper has a lively interest in maintaining the candidates' operational expertise. And while the Republicans too often have to depend upon volunteer help, the helper from the union knows that in many instances his job is on the line, so he'd better get out there and do whatever job the union boss tells him to perform.

Creating Inflation and Unemployment

Because of its influence on lawmakers, the great power amassed by organized labor over the past years has contributed mightily to the recent runaway inflation and unemployment. It enabled unions to get wage increases for workers far in excess of their increased productivity. In other words, because of the immunity now enjoyed by the unions, its members have stopped working harder to obtain benefits.

Federal Trade Commissioner Mayo Thompson believes if the average American was willing to work productively enough to raise our real output by 5, 8, or 10 percent a year, we could all have a corresponding increase in our individual incomes without inflation or higher rates of unemployment.

Thompson says the choice is: Settle for a 3 percent increase in wages and other forms of income, or buckle down and work harder.

But he sees trouble in labor unions that claim to speak for government workers. "Either we break the power of unions to demand and get wage increases in excess of our productivity growth-rate," he says, "or we're going to have inflation and unemployment into all the foreseeable future."

Thompson argues, and I agree with him, that we are strangling the incentive to work in this country with a maze of labor and welfare laws that "take away too much of the carrot, and virtually all of the stick." All we have to do is look at Britain, he says, adding: "There you have a prime example of what is happening here."

Treat Big Unions Like Big Business

I agree fully with Commissioner Thompson when he points out that the time when America's trade unions resided in run-down headquarters to wage the battle for union benefits belongs to the 1930's. Now most of them operate out of beautiful marble edifices, such as the one the money-heavy Teamsters Union maintains within walking distance of the U.S. Capitol. There is absolutely no reason why labor organizations that can build such large, mausoleum-type headquarters buildings in Washington should be given special treatment by the government. Instead, big labor is far better able to comply with the laws governing American corporation themselves.

And why the unions should be exempted from meeting the provisions of the nation's antitrust laws I have never been able to understand. There may once have been a time when that made some sense from an economic standpoint. But that time was passed long ago when unions became big business.

CONCLUSIONS

Power Brokers in the Congress

The pursuit of power in government goes on unabated, even though most American problems can be traced to the abuse of the authority which should belong to the people. It's like a contagious disease which has run a disastrous course in the executive branch of government and is now beginning to infect the Congress.

The chairmen of committees and subcommittees of the Senate and House, as well as their staffs, appear to be superconscious of the power they wield over important legislation. They seem determined to regulate the lives and activities of American citizens in almost every area of human endeavor. Since 1962 the Congress has passed more than twenty-five measures calling for new regulations on the American people and American business, and these programs have increased the costs, the paperwork, and the inflationary pressures on the entire nation.

Meanwhile, power brokers in the Senate and House have used their influence to grind axes for special interests they favor. For example, at the end of the 93rd Congress I was witness to the procedure used to write some tax loopholes into law. It went like this:

Within the last few hours of the session, Chairman Russell Long of the Senate Finance Committee called up a bill which all the Senate members thought had to do solely with providing some relief for the families of veterans, since its title was as tender as a mother's love—"To Provide Tax Relief to the Families of Prisoners of War of Our Fighting Men Listed as Missing in Action." Naturally, every member with an ounce of compassion would want to vote for such a bill.

I know I did—that is, until I got a look at the twelve committee amendments that had somehow gotten attached to the POW tax bill. I found they had nothing to do with the main title or the subject of the bill, but were instead tax loopholes carved out especially for preferred people. One extended to distilled spirits brought into the United States from Puerto Rico and the Virgin Islands—the same refund provisions, in the case of loss or destruction, that are presently applicable to imported or domestic spirits.

This is a typical example of how some committee chairmen work. The bill had remained on the calendar from July 8 but was not called up until the last moments of the session in late December when it was believed that not many members would be in attendance and the ones remaining would be anxious to leave.

The point I want to make is this: Those amendments could not have been added to the bill without the knowledge of the committee's chairman because they were committee amendments. But they were added and the Senate was all set to approve them until I objected.

Here we have a small group of men with a flair for getting re-elected and a desire for power that can make a mockery on Capitol Hill of the concept of a representative democracy. These are men who run the Congress. They are the chairmen of almost every important committee and subcommittee of the Senate and House. They decide what bills should be contained in every bill submitted for action.

They can ignore bills referred to their committee or they can go through the motions of considering them; that is, give the bills a couple of days of hearings, follow that with a staff report that takes many weeks to write, and then forget the whole thing.

All Power Can Be Misused

When I think about how government bureaucracies operate, I am always reminded of that fine segment in John F. Kennedy's inaugural speech, when he said, "Ask not what your country can do for you but what you can do for your country." Washington is full of groups or individuals that are forever coming up with ways in which the country can do to you or for you with your money. Those interested in reform should demand an end to this now before our lives are totally dominated by Washington.

Before closing, I would like to re-emphasize that when power is used to deprive people of their freedoms, it makes no difference where it accumulated. This is what I have attempted to show in these pages.

Power lodged in hidden recesses of government and vested in unknown bureaucrats can sometimes be as important as that wielded by a heavily partisan Congress or a power-hungry president. It is the power *per se*—the authority—the official influence —that counts.

How Far Have Things Gone?

As I worked on the manuscript, it became clear to me that the great majority of the American people have no accurate picture whatsoever of just what is going on in their government. They are totally unaware of the coming breakpoint. Let me give a few statistics that, hopefully, may shock some readers into a realization of how far things have gone in the Republic.

For every dollar we paid in income tax in 1976, the government borrowed fifty cents. Two hundred years ago the United States began this process—and here I'm talking about borrowing —to win their freedom. At that time we borrowed $8 million to finance our revolution.

Today that debt is 76,000 times greater. It is being used for a phenomenal increase in the cost of operating the Congress and implementing the sweeping powers given to that faceless army making up the regulatory agencies which tell the American people what they can and cannot do in most of the important areas of their everyday lives. The debt is being used to finance a growing, unworkable, and destructive welfare system which has not solved any problems—but has created many. And it is increasing the threat of a breakpoint.

The increased debt, of course, defrays the cost of the greatest bureaucracy—with all of its waste, inefficiency, and duplication —the world has ever seen. It pays for a government work force (federal) of 2,800,000 people, the largest salaried group anywhere in the nation or in the world. The increasing machinery helps account for some of the $16 billion a year required just to handle the federal government's paperwork "blizzard" for one year.

More and more I believe that we are in a period which Thomas Jefferson would have described as one requiring a revolution to restore the principles of the American Revolution. In his inaugural address, Jefferson called for a return to the Spirit of 1776, and said the general government must be preserved in "its whole Constitutional vigor, as the sheet anchor of our peace at home and our safety abroad."

Although Jefferson was referring to situations that existed in the United States of his day, I believe there is in his words a strain of wisdom that is more applicable to our present state of affairs than most statements I keep hearing in Washington. In fact, I think it is safe to say that more so now than at any other time in our history, we need revolutionary thinking and acting in respect to all segments of government if we are to avoid the breakpoint.

Ten Years Before the Breakpoint

Is the United States doomed to collapse under the weight of deficits resulting from the long contest for power in the federal government?

I certainly don't think the Damoclean threat is immediate, but I do think the nation has less than ten years to function at the current rate of expenditures before the sword descends. I also believe the country is in for some very rough times because of federal economic stupidity.

As I stated at the start, my primary reason for writing this work is to alert Americans to the dangers of power concentrated in any place or in any hands. It is not, to repeat what I've often said during my political career, the concentration of power in foreign countries or any combination of foreign countries that I fear, but the power within our own government's structure that slowly but surely undermines the morality of the people and even their ability to understand what is happening to their freedom before it is all gone. The wrong use of power has destroyed more governments and deprived more people of freedom than has any other action in the history of man. Throughout the course of this work, I have mentioned only a few of the abuses that I see from the nation's capitol. It has been sort of like skimming the top of the milk; the real substance is way down underneath. I have cited facts and figures, but hundreds of thousands remain unrecorded here. Some rather bizarre and unusual incidents have been noted, but thousands more exist.

If this does nothing more than whet your appetite for finding out more about the abusive power that has grown in Washington since the early 1930's, then I will consider it a success. It is only when the American people finally come to realize what is happening to the freedoms they have always taken for granted, to the monies they have worked so hard to earn, and to the moral atmosphere of our nation as a result of these abuses that any change will take place in the structure of Congress, so that enough courage can be shown to redirect the course of history which is now headed, in my humble opinion, toward total disaster.

Rome Before the Collapse

One of the best suggestions I could make to anyone who has proceeded this far is that he go back through the works of Gibbon to where he discusses the decline and fall of the Roman Empire. Or for even easier reading, some of the historical novels by Taylor Caldwell describe the conditions in Rome prior to its collapse. This will give the reader an understanding of what conservatives mean when they stress the admonition, previously quoted, that is inscribed on Washington's National Archives Building: "What is past is prologue—study the past." If we will remember the lessons of history, we can prevent the disasters of history from repeating themselves.

It has taken the United States many years to get into a position where its power so absolutely dominates so many factors of our lives; curtailing that power is not going to be an overnight venture. As matters stand now, we are in about the same position as was Rome before she collapsed, in the same position that Babylon and ancient Greece and the modern countries of Europe found themselves before the freedoms of the people and the powers of the countries disappeared. Some people, in fact too many, go blithely on their way thinking it can't happen here. They have never heard of the breakpoint.

"Old Glory" or Past Glory

Thus in spite of the fact that Old Glory is still a symbol of everything we hold dear and great in this country, in spite of the fact that every time the flag is paraded down the streets of our towns and cities it brings men to attention and tears to the eyes of those who care—in spite of all of this, the American flag and all it stands for can fall. It can go down even though for two hundred years men have been willing to lay down their lives for the freedoms God has given us and which our constitutional government was set up to protect.

All the way from Valley Forge through the bitterness of the war between the States, through the terrors of World Wars I and II, Korea, and Vietnam, our men have added to the glory of the flag and to the perpetuation and protection of our freedom. The colonists, the pioneers who opened up our frontiers, the men and women who tilled the soil, and those who created our cities—all these were people who cherished that hard-won freedom and consequently resisted any offers of so-called government help that would chip away at it. Instead, they depended on their own hard work and personal initiative to make what they wanted out of their lives.

This is the kind of glory that built our nation. It is the kind of glory on which we prided ourselves and through which we became mighty throughout the entire world. But despite the triumph of the people over power in the past, the present curses and threats to freedom will not automatically pass. Once men have felt the strength of power they are not likely to give it up voluntarily. It will, I repeat, have to be taken away from them and placed back where it was supposed to reside, and this will happen only when the American people find the courage to elect Congressess that don't hold out glittering promises which, when implemented, simply increase the concentration of bureaucratic power and entangle the people in an even tighter web of dependency on the government. Saying "No" to any more government "benefits" may mean that our present standard of living will have to be lowered a bit. But if we don't settle for a little less now, we most assuredly will be forced to settle for a great deal less in the not-too-distant future.

American Is Worth Fighting For

Now, as we begin our third century I think the challenge that faces us all is whether Americans will celebrate the 225th, 250th, 300th, or 500th anniversaries of this country. Or will our children be looking back on the ruins of a once-great concept that died because not enough people cared?

Recently a friend of mine told me that in his stamp-collecting days he purchased an English stamp which carried the familiar slogan, "The sun never sets on the British Empire." But the sun has set on the empire because England allowed herself to become weak, militarily as well as economically. The question that this brings to mind is: Just where is our sun in relation to the United States? Is it at high noon where it should be? Or is it over the yardarm, ready to disappear beyond the horizon?

If darkness comes, it will be because the United States has lost both its economic and military strength. Our sun can begin to set without external influence. All that is necessary to bring about such a tragedy is the continued apathy of American business people, professionals, and individual citizens coupled with the unbridled power of government bureaucracies, the labor unions and special-interest groups.

To sum up, my purpose has been to give the reader and the American public some idea of what this one elected official sees taking place within the structure of our government; for just as surely as I'm writing this, the bureaucratic meddling in our lives can destroy our God-given freedoms and the government set up to protect them almost two hundred years ago. Again, I hope I'm wrong in my pessimism, but history, I'm afraid, could well prove me right. If you have read anything that you find disturbing, I would suggest you discuss it with your neighbors and friends, because only when the American people are aware of what is taking place will they demand change.

Believe me, I know from past experience that when the people get wrought up over a public issue such as runaway federal spending, they make it known to their representatives and senators in Congress. And also believe me when I say that when this happens, you get action from the liberal mandarins who control the Senate and House.

That's what we need right now, so let's get cracking. We have nothing to lose but an army of petty dictators ordering us how to live. The American way of life is at stake, and that's worth fighting for. If we join together in the fight, we can still avoid reaching the breakpoint.

SECTION

2

ABOUT CARL KARCHER

Carl N. Karcher is founder and president of Carl Karcher Enterprises, Inc., a west coast food service chain operating approximately 225 restaurants in California—one of the nation's largest, privately owned restaurant chains.

Carl believes that success in any endeavor is rooted in the enjoyment of doing it and, in business, that enjoyment lies in making it work better for a stronger and more prosperous America. He believes that if government leaves it alone, private enterprise has the built-in requisites, and incentives, to produce the earnings needed to create the new jobs for America's growing work force. He has demonstrated his beliefs by his own exciting performance.

Beginning with a nest-egg of just $326, one hot dog stand, and total consecration to the code of self-reliance, he now presides over a work force of 6,500 happy and secure people, contributing to the support and strength of their country. His goal is to create 1,500 new jobs each year. With 1,500,000 new job seekers coming on stream every year, it appears that what the country needs is not more government-made jobs, created by more deficit spending and inflation, but 1,000 Carl Karchers with freedom to make free enterprise work.

Carl's philosophy is reflected in his daily life that begins in the early morning and continues late into the night. In addition to the enormous responsibility of running a major business, he finds the time to devote to the leadership of many community activities, charities, and to winning converts to a better understanding of the inter-dependence of free enterprise and a secure and prosperous America.

THE RIGHT OF PRIVATE ENTERPRISE TO BE FREE TO PRODUCE THE PROFITS WHICH CREATE THE NEW JOBS THAT SPAWN PROSPERITY FOR ALL.

By CARL N. KARCHER

I never cease to be perplexed over why so few people understand how their own fortunes are directly related to the ability of American business to earn consistent and healthy profits.

It is so simple. We are all in this game of making a living together—striving to improve our lot within a system called private enterprise, which means employers and employees in search of profit (employees think of it as savings.)

Because business profit is the seed corn of job-growth, and high employment the key to national prosperity, everyone has a stake in a thriving business climate.

Every business must earn profits if it is to grow, or even survive. Growth is another word for expansion and expansion creates the need for new workers. But expansion must be justified, and largely financed, by the accumulation of earnings beyond the cost of doing business —in other words, profits.

Conversely, when business losses replace earnings, companies must lay off workers in order to stay alive. That triggers a spiral of unemployment because the unemployed don't buy the products that other companies make; government revenues shrink in proportion to the loss of taxes on disappearing profits and wages, while government deficit spending goes up to care for the unemployed.

Thus, fears are engendered that cause people, generally, to spend less, which is destructive to the profits of other businesses who must, in turn, lay off some of their workers, and the vicious cycle of rising unemployment, lower tax revenues and higher government deficit spending begins. A recession sets in and everybody suffers.

Business profits, after governments (city, state and federal) take about half in taxes, are the lowest in years—less than 5% of sales, on the average. United States Senator William Proxmire, certainly no apologist for big business, recently made these perceptive comments according to a bulletin of Mobil Oil:

"Somehow the impression has developed in this country that corporate profits have been excessive. The fact is they have not been... profits in relation to other income have been in a steady decline for 25 years. Profits are now about half as large a proportion of wages and salaries as they were 25 years ago... profits are what drives this great economy ... if profits are too low our economy cannot engender the capital essential for good jobs and an abundance of what we need for the good life."

To offer an illustration of how business earnings are the direct catalyst which creates jobs, let me cite the history of Carl Karcher Enterprises, of which I am priveleged to be founder and president. We own and operate a chain of over 225 fast-food and conventional restaurants in California—the second largest privately owned, non-franchised restaurant chain in the United States.

We started with one hot dog stand and one employee 37 years ago—made a profit and invested it in another stand and another employee. We repeated that over and over again, always plowing profits back into growth, until today we employ 6500 people—all due to the freedom and opportunity to earn and utilize profits. And these 6500 people (who probably support another 6500) are all tax "payers," not tax consumers! We have now set as our goal the engendering of 1500 new jobs a year.

Private enterprise in search of profit is what makes our system work, and our system fills the wants and needs of people better than any other, anywhere in the world.

It is so clear to me that government, business and workers all share a common interest of creating the "good life" for themselves and their families—a condition of mutual interdependence, so to speak—that I cannot understand the prevalence of acrimony that is so pervasive between them; or the sorry exhibition of some media people going on television, with misinformation, to stir up animosity against the oil industry that must generate, and risk, billions of dollars to develop the new sources of energy that the nation so desperately needs. And, incidentally, you can't drill new holes in the ground, or beneath the sea, without putting more people to work.

According to former Treasury Secretary William E. Simon, government bureaucracy inflicts a penalty of $125 billion a year on American business through "unnecessary" regulations. This includes some $40 billion as the cost of the mountain of forms that the bureaucrats demand be filled out and sent to Washington—a large proportion of which they can't possibly utilize. And government is dependent upon business profits and employed people for its revenues! (For revelations on this subject be sure to read the startling condensa-

tion of Senator Goldwater's latest book. THE COMING BREAKPOINT, appearing as Section I of this book.

Secondly, too many labor unions are in constant battle with management to procure a bigger and bigger slice of the owners' receipts without assuring proportionately higher worker productivity, which must accompany higher wages and benefits if our system is to work without setting off more inflation. They are seemingly unaware of the probability that their demands will impede the company's capability to grow and create the new jobs that growth generates.

Both emulate the spectacle of a man choking himself—or, killing the goose that lays the golden eggs.

In the nature of things, the business of business is generating jobs. America needs 1,500,000 new ones every year to keep pace with the growing work force. The only way these new jobs will be spawned is for American business to be set free to generate enough earnings to expand its production and hire the additional workers that will then be needed. So, in effect, no profits, no growth. No growth, no jobs.

It is a simple truth that people who snipe at profits are unwittingly taking pot shots at their own jobs, their governments' tax revenues and, in the end, their own standard of living.

If, instead, we will all recognize that it is the great engine of private enterprise that built this nation, and if we will work together toward making it less difficult for the engine to generate steady profits, we can all look forward to a healthier economy, a decline of inflation, a more productive and happier people, and even, perhaps, a nation that is solvent once again.

The messages which follow, originated and published by the Warner & Swasey Company, Cleveland, Ohio, shed further light on the meaning and the rewards of that unique American invention—free competitive enterprise, working for a stronger and more secure republic.

Carl Karcher

You can't kill profit until you've killed freedom

EVEN if you abolished the profit-and-loss system in America and installed it in Russia, in a short while it would be back in America and dead in Russia. The profit-and-loss system is not something you decide to have or not have — it is something that can't help but arise in a country which has liberty — it grows in liberty just as surely as grain grows in sunshine.

When you are free, the human desire to improve your lot and that of your family shows itself. To improve your own lot, you have to do something better than others do it. If you succeed, you benefit (make a profit) and in the process you benefit the public, too. If you do not succeed, you don't benefit but you can always try again if you have the character.

In this act of *expressing your liberty* you have *created* the profit-and-loss system. Liberty made you free to work in your best way . . . to be enterprising. Maybe that's why it's called "free enterprise."

"The fifth freedom — the freedom of individual enterprise — is the keystone upon which the other four freedoms rests. In our system, the four cannot survive the fall of the fifth."

— Nicholas Murray Butler

"The worst crime against working people is a company which fails to operate at a profit"

A GREAT labor leader made this statement. He knew that unless a company can make money it will be forced out of business — and an idle factory supplies no jobs; a prosperous factory supplies more and more jobs at better and better pay.

Three groups share equally the much discussed responsibility for jobs:

1 — **Government.** Its regulations and tax laws must enable companies to save enough money to provide workmen with constantly improved equipment without which this country can never compete in the world-wide competition for trade.

2 — **Management.** It must provide the improved equipment, and honestly share with its workmen the increased earnings which result.

3 — **Labor.** It must use the equipment efficiently because a man can be paid only out of what he produces. Therefore, if he wants to earn more, he must produce more, efficiently — and improved equipment is the only way he can do it.

Government can't legislate jobs, management can't invent them, labor can't force them . . . but all three, *working together,* can develop them.

Pencil sketch of Samuel Gompers, father of the American labor movement, by Enrico Caruso in 1914. Courtesy of Library of Congress.

Doing for people what they can and ought to do for themselves is a dangerous experiment. In the last analysis, the welfare of the workers depends upon their own initiative. Whatever is done under the guise of philanthropy or social morality which in any way lessens initiative is the greatest crime that can be committed against the toilers. Let social busybodies and professional "public morals experts" in their fads reflect upon the perils they rashly invite under this pretense of social welfare.

—Samuel Gompers

77

"No wage is too high if the worker earns it. 5¢ an hour is too high if the worker doesn't earn it"

ONE OF the most staunch friends labor ever had made that statement. He knew wages can come only from production, and an increase can come only from *increased* production.

Guidelines are not set for long by governments; they are set by *consumers,* and when unearned higher wages force prices higher (as they must, and are now doing) the customer simply stops buying. And then more and more workers have no wage at all.

"28¢ profit out of each $1 of sales is too high"

—says the typical American. We agree. When that same American is asked "what is a *fair* return" he says 10¢ out of each dollar.

The *actual* return to corporations is 4¢. And without adequate profit there's not enough money to buy new machines to keep American-made goods competitive with low cost foreign goods—or else American factory jobs will continue to disappear.

"Society is always taken by surprise at
any new example of common sense."
— Ralph Waldo Emerson

"Productivity" is a long word for an easier job

"COMBATING inflation with greater productivity" sounds like producing more by working harder for longer hours.

Wrong.

Greater and better productivity is simply using more modern skills and machines to produce more and better products easier, that sell better for less money — and so pay workers and machine owners more, and make their jobs and companies safer.

We need an easier word for "productivity" — and more people who understand its true meaning.

Early production line of Ford Motor Company, which introduced the concept of how mass production produces more goods, more jobs, and at lesser costs.

When a Company dies everyone pays for the funeral

THE successful company benefits not only its owners but everyone — it carries its part of the tax load, provides more and better jobs, supplies goods at a fair price to the public. *Everyone benefits.*

The unsuccessful company provides fewer and fewer jobs and no opportunities for young workers. It pays less and less share of taxes. It cannot afford research to improve its products and values. It finally dies and so provides *no* jobs, *no* taxes, *no* future for workers, *no* values for anyone.

Isn't it wise, then, for tax laws and labor leaders to work with management to do everything possible for business success?

CLOSED
UNTIL FURTHER
NOTICE

The biggest dividend
profits pay is jobs

IN one American company there are 36,000 employees making and selling new products which that company has developed within the past 25 years.

Those new products are the result of the company's own research paid for out of the company's profits. Is there anything wrong with that? Remember: no profits, no research. No research, no 36,000 new jobs.

Yet this is one of the companies which has been bitterly attacked by government.

Why? What do we want in this country — more power for Washington, or more jobs for American workmen?

"There is far more danger in public than in private monoply. For when government goes into business it can always shift its losses to the people. For government never makes ends meet, while that is the first requisite of business."

—Thomas A. Edison

American business can sell anything except its most important product — ITSELF

THE most important thing in America today to the safety and well-being of every American is solvent, healthy American business.

When business is sick, all America is sick — charity and education shrink, wages disappear for millions, savings evaporate, young people get no jobs, opportunities and hope disappear, neighborhoods sink into slums.

When business is prosperous there are more and more jobs, charity is extended, more profits produce more taxes for more education and other good uses, opportunities increase for all the young, modern housing gets built.

That's how vital healthy, prosperous business is to the well-being of all America. But you don't often hear American businessmen pointing out that fact.

They'd better.

SECTION

3

ABOUT HARRY F. BYRD, JR.

A distinguished American of a distinguished American family, Senator Harry F. Byrd, Jr. of Virginia carries on in the tradition of his father, the famed U.S. Senator and publisher, and his uncle, Admiral Richard E. Byrd, the Arctic explorer. Like his father, Senator Byrd is deeply concerned with government deficit spending.

He was executive officer of a Navy patrol bombing squadron in the Pacific during World War II, and spent 18 years in the Virginia Senate prior to his appointment to the U.S. Senate in 1965. He was returned to the Senate as a Democrat in 1966 and re-elected as an "Independent" in 1970 and 1976.

One of the Senate giants, bucking the tide of reckless federal spending and controls over American life, Senator Byrd says, "Congress itself is greatly to blame for the condition in which the government finds its finances today . . . I cannot see that Congress is making any effective effort to get spending under control." No one in the Senate is working harder, or accomplishing more, to bring runaway government growth and deficits under control. He finishes his stirring messages on a note of hope.

THE RIGHT TO INVOKE THE 10TH AMENDMENT—RESTORATION OF GOVERNING POWERS RESERVED TO THE STATES AND THE PEOPLE

By U.S. SENATOR HARRY F. BYRD, JR.

No provision of the Constitution is more critical to the preservation of our liberties than the Tenth Amendment. Its language is straightforward:

"The powers not delegated to the United States by the Constitution, nor prohibited by it to the States, are reserved to the States respectively, or to the people."

In my judgement, the Tenth Amendment to the Constitution is being distorted. Too much power is being concentrated in Washington; too many powers and responsibilities reserved to the States by the Constitution are being usurped by the federal government.

I am reminded of the conversation I had a quarter of a century ago with one whom I believe is the greatest man of the 20th century, Winston Churchill. I spent a delightful day with Mr. Churchill at his office in the House of Commons and many things stick in my mind about our lengthy discussions. But none is more vivid than our dialogue regarding the relative merits of the British Parliamentary system and the American Constitutional system.

At one point I made the comment that the British system in some respects had much to commend it over the American. I shall never forget Mr. Churchill's reply:

"Ah, yes, Mr. Byrd," he said, "but then don't forget that the basic strength of America lies in the fact that the people of the 48 states acting through their own legislatures, can to a very considerable extent, determine their own destinies. You, in America, are not centralized like we are in England."

To me, this great statesman 3,000 miles from our shores recognized and proclaimed the importance of the tenth amendment to our constitution, the purpose of which is to reserve fundamental rights to the individual states, and thus, to the people.

The Englishman, John Locke, taught that power must be restrained, and in France, the legal philosopher Montesquieu wrote:

"Every man invested with power is apt to abuse it."

In America, James Madison sounded the same theme: "All men having power," he said, "ought to be mistrusted."

Blunt words, revolutionary words—but words upon which a just government might, at last, be erected.

Thomas Jefferson saw the mistrust of power as the keystone of constitutionalism. In a statement which I feel should be engraved in stone in the Senate, the House of Representatives, the Supreme Court and the Oval Office of the White House, Jefferson declared:

"In questions of power, let no more be heard of confidence in man, but bind him down from mischief by the chains of the Constitution."

If power derives from the people, and if those in power must be restrained, then the law itself must be supreme. Equally important— and this is the theme of the Tenth Amendment—power must *not* be concentrated in the hands of a few.

In the early days of the Republic, no president—indeed, not the whole federal government —could present any real threat to individual liberty or the rights of the states. Yet Jefferson foresaw the consequences of future concentration of power. He articulated the basic American belief, central to our whole history, that power *concentrated* sooner or later becomes power abused.

We are witnessing today the consequences of too long a neglect of Jefferson's wisdom. We see decisions of enormous importance to the whole nation handed down by a remote and faceless bureaucracy in Washington. In recent years, the government in Washington has spun a giant web of regulation that reaches aspects of every business and industry and lives of all our citizens. The *Federal Register,* the journal of new federal regulations and legal notices, published over 60,000 pages in 1976.

With regulation this extensive, it is next to impossible to keep track of what the law *is*— let alone comply with it.

All his life, Thomas Jefferson warned of the dangers of over-centralized power. In a letter written 13 years after he had left the Presidency, Jefferson stated:

"When all government, in little as in great things, shall be drawn to Washington as the center of all power, it will render powerless the checks provided of one government on another . . ."

Now the first thing that strikes me about those words of Jefferson's is their farsightedness. Indeed, they are prophetic. Power was not, in Jefferson's day, "drawn to Washington." Our first presidents were leaders of a nation truly diverse in character; state and local governments vigorously asserted their autonomy; and the country lacked the rapid transportation and communication network which, even as it draws us together today, also created opportunities for exploitation of power pressures and conformity.

The constitution represents the supreme law of our land. It was devised by great and wise men to protect our liberties for all time. We must either adhere to it scrupulously, and in total, or accept its crumbling away—a consequence that will surely follow the erosion of any of its parts, and with it the loss of liberty.

In terms of the Tenth Amendment, and the spending power crisis at the federal level today, a clear demand is beginning for a reverse flow of power from Washington—a systematic transfer of authority and tax money to the state and local levels for those programs that can best be watched and administered on the "home front." Our nation of 215 million people and 3 million square miles is too large and diverse to be run from Washington.

Some broad areas that should be tackled first are welfare, education, housing, food stamps, and scores of foolish federal grants now coming out of Washington. The result of such "home town" responsibility would be to soon expose the cheaters, eliminate duplication and waste, greatly reduce costs (taxes) and channel public aid to those most in need and deserving. It simply means getting the people directly involved by turning their own problems over to them to solve. If we do, believe me, they will get the job done and we will see federal deficits and needless bureaucracies melt away like snow before a spring thaw.

Let me cite a true story and example of "local action" as reported by James W. Kofski of the Associated Press, and appearing in the Reader's Digest issue of March, 1977:

"The little town of Faith, South Dakota, has turned down a $200,000 federal grant for a new grandstand at the Faith Stock Show and Rodeo Grounds. 'We've got to refuse these grants or there isn't going to be a U.S.A. for our kids and grandkids' said Don King, vice president of the Stock Show and Rodeo. 'There's just too much doggone wasted money' added Mayor Ron Bachman. What irked the townspeople was not that they were required to put up $50,000, but that of the government's matching $200,000, only $87,500 would go for materials. The rest would go for labor and 'administrative expenses.' The Stock Show Board voted unanimously to buy the materials with the $50,000 they were asked to raise and then do the job the way they usually do in Faith—on their own."

I believe the American people are sick and tired of excessive regulation by big government. They want to return to the limited government envisioned by Jefferson—and they are letting the officials in Washington know what they want.

Slowly but surely, I believe the message is getting through. I think there is real hope of reversing the long trend toward ever-bigger deficits and ever-widening regulation. The people must have a greater voice in government and government must have a lesser role in the lives of the people. Let us affirm our faith in individual liberty—the faith which created our country. I believe this can be done.

To return once more to words of Jefferson, let us recall that he said:

"We are always equal to what we undertake with resolution . . . it is part of the American character to consider nothing as desperate; to surmount every difficulty by resolution and contrivance."

In that spirit, let us move forward to a "Rebirth of our Nation" through a rebirth of the meaning of the Tenth Amendment.

"The political liberal is usually he who
is liberal with someone else's money."
— Senator Carter Glass

Before you vote for any man, make sure he knows how to subtract

ALL politicians seem to be wizards at addition — they can add government employees without batting an eye, add give-away programs, add to deficits and debt. That's easy — it doesn't cost them anything, and it gets some careless votes.

But the politicians who can save this country from collapse and bankruptcy are the *statesmen* who know how to subtract needless government employees, how to subtract programs and bureaus we can live without, how to subtract 100% from our deficit so that we can begin to subtract from Federal, State and local debts which are crushing this country.

Let's start by doing some subtracting on our own — subtract all the Big Spenders from office.

That dishonorable, anti-American excuse— "If I don't get it, somebody else will."

CITIZENS, mayors, governors, U.S. Congressmen clamber to get on the Federal Funds bandwagon that is wrecking the character and the future of America.

There is no such thing as Federal funds—every dollar is local taxation collected by Washington and then *some* (but only some) is doled out (after the bureaucrats take theirs) to local governments in exchange for local freedom.

When is some local official or unit going to have the courage, the common sense, the honesty to say NO to the lure of "Federal" funds, and to say with pride, "We'll pay our own way, and if we can't afford it, we'll wait until we can."

Then, pray Heaven, there will be enough honest Americans left to follow that leader—back to solvency and honesty and self-respect again.

Robbing St. Petersburg
to pay St. Paul

WHY should I expect *you* to pay my bills? Yet that is what "Federal" funds mean.

It may be all very well for Florida, for example, in its generosity to give St. Paul a new Auditorium or some shiny transit system. But don't call it *Federal* money because it isn't — there *is* no Federal money. It all comes from Florida and New York and California — *and St. Paul* which sends its taxes to Washington where 2,800,000 Federal employees must take out their "handling charges," and send back what's left, cluttered and hamstrung with Federal restrictions.

If St. Paul (and every city and state) would meet its own needs by paying its own bills under its own management, those bills would be far lower, and the money would be better spent.

Depressed areas
stay depressed

BECAUSE the Federal government *takes* too much money *from* them, not because it doesn't *give* enough *to* them.

For the hundredth time we say, the Federal government has no money it does not first take away from the states. Why not leave it there in the first place? Less of it would be needed because less would be wasted.

Bureaucrats build no roads, teach no schools, erect no housing, care for no old or sick. Only local money, mostly from the areas where the schools and houses and roads and old people are, can do that — local money, or what's left of it, when it gets back home from its costly trip to Washington.

"A government has no wealth, and when a politician promises to give you something for nothing, he must first confiscate that wealth from you."
— Rep. Bill Dickinson (D-Ala

by M. Welman

"You never had it so good"
(until you read the fine print)

TAX CUTS and maybe more to come — higher and higher wages and now shorter hours, too . . . bigger social security . . . free education for your children . . . free medical care . . . and the government will be your conscience to take care of the poor so you won't have to concern yourself about anything.

Hallelujah! It's wonderful!

But just who do you think is going to pay for all this — Santa Claus? The Easter rabbit? You know perfectly well the government has to collect in taxes all it spends *plus* the government handling charge. So when you buy any product or service you have to pay your share of all those fancy government programs. That wasn't in the noble speeches which authorized the billions, but the billions have to be paid, so they're added to the prices you pay now — or they're borrowed and so added to the prices you pay tomorrow.

But you pay. And pay. And pay.

When we're giving away money we don't have, and getting hatred and antagonism in return... when we're borrowing money at high interest in order to give more money away... when we have to raise our debt limit to 750 billion dollars in order to continue pouring our billions all over the world — then isn't it time you and I told Congress what they have *got to do* — STOP SPENDING, AND *SAVE.*

Here's the sorry, tragic record — our "loans" and give-aways (which we couldn't afford) 1946 to 1974.

Afghanistan	$463,900,000
Bangladesh	525,600,000
Cyprus	29,500,000
Egypt	891,600,000
Greece	4,253,300,000
India	9,026,400,000
Iran	2,129,100,000
Iraq	93,300,000
Israel	5,204,500,000
Jordan	1,084,200,000
Lebanon	151,000,000
Nepal	198,600,000
Pakistan	4,982,400,000
Saudi Arabia	326,500,000
Sri Lanka	214,300,000
Syria	61,200,000
Turkey	6,608,600,000
Yeman, People's Democratic Republic of	4,500,000
Yemen Arab Republic	50,000,000
Central Treaty Organization	52,700,000
*Near East and South Asia Regional	459,000,000
Argentina	394,800,000
Bahamas	300,000
Barbados	1,200,000
Belize	6,900,000
Bolivia	663,900,000
Brazil	2,913,800,000
Chile	1,125,800,000
Colombia	1,424,700,000
Costa Rica	199,800,000
Cuba	16,400,000
Dominican Republic	520,800,000
Ecuador	345,600,000
El Salvador	162,500,000
Guatamala	329,400,000
Guyana	80,400,000
Haiti	121,300,000
Honduras	169,700,000
Jamaica	99,800,000
Mexico	297,900,000
Nicaragua	223,700,000
Panama	317,000,000
Paraguay	167,500,000
Peru	598,000,000
Surinam	5,800,000
Trinidad and Tobago	40,500,000
Uruguay	210,300,000
Venezuela	340,300,000
Other West Indies	13,000,000
ROCAP	247,800,000
*East Caribbean Regional	33,000,000
Latin America Regional	3,192,400,000
Burma	185,000,000
Cambodia	1,799,400,000
China, Republic of	5,708,500,000
Hong Kong	43,800,000
Indochina, Undistributed	1,542,500,000
Indonesia	1,991,500,000
Japan	3,834,100,000
Korea	11,360,500,000
Laos	2,521,700,000
Malaysia	131,000,000
Philippines	2,355,600,000
Ryukyu Islands	413,700,000
Singapore	23,500,000
Thailand	1,898,600,000
Vietnam	22,356,300,000
Western Samoa	4,000,000
East Asia Regional	422,700,000

we're broke!

Algeria	180,400,000
Botswana	33,900,000
Burundi	10,300,000
Cameroon	34,400,000
Central African Republic	6,800,000
Chad	17,900,000
Congo, People's Republic of the	5,600,000
Dahomey	15,600,000
Ethiopia	538,400,000
Gabon	7,800,000
The Gambia	7,100,000
Ghana	283,300,000
Guinea	105,900,000
Ivory Coast	35,900,000
Kenya	112,000,000
Lesotho	19,000,000
Liberia	229,700,000
*Libya	228,600,000
Malagasy Republic	15,900,000
Malawi	30,700,000
Mali, Republic of	52,400,000
*Mauritania	16,400,000
Mauritius	12,900,000
Morocco	938,800,000
Niger	47,200,000
Nigeria	410,100,000
Rwanda	8,800,000
Senegal	52,000,000
Seychelles	500,000
Sierra Leone	44,800,000
Somali Republic	77,100,000
*South Africa, Republic of	1,300,000
*Southern Rhodesia	7,000,000
Sudan	120,600,000
Swaziland	7,700,000
Tanzania	94,800,000
Togo	22,900,000
Tunisia	799,500,000
Uganda	42,900,000
Upper Volta	34,100,000
Zaire	501,900,000
*Zambia	33,800,000
Central and West Africa Regional	115,700,000
East Africa Regional	34,300,000
Southern Africa Regional	56,400,000
Africa Regional	246,000,000
Albania	20,400,000
Austria	1,251,200,000
*Belgium-Luxembourg	1,853,100,000
Czechoslovakia	193,000,000
Denmark	907,800,000
Finland	56,900,000
*France	8,273,500,000
German Democratic Republic	800,000
*Germany (Federal Republic)	4,979,300,000
Berlin	131,900,000
*Hungary	32,700,000
Iceland	82,000,000
Ireland	146,500,000
*Italy	5,688,800,000
Malta	43,200,000
*Netherlands	2,282,800,000
*Norway	1,216,200,000
*Poland	539,300,000
Portugal	505,700,000
Romania	9,700,000
Spain	1,882,800,000
*Sweden	109,000,000
United Kingdom	8,730,800,000
U.S.S.R.	186,400,000
Yugoslavia	2,747,400,000
Europe Regional	835,800,000
*Australia	123,600,000
*New Zealand	8,600,000
Papua New Guinea	300,000
*Trust Territory of the Pacific Ialands	528,600,000
Other Oceania	9,800,000
*Canada	30,600,000
Interregional	15,334,500,000
Grand Total	$172,109,000,000

Source: Agency for International Development, U.S. State Department

Loans only (3.6 billion) repaid in full with interest. Some other countries have made partial payments on their loans totaling $14.8 billion including interest.

101

THE REWARDS OF WORK
By Lawrence Welk

I believe my views about our American free enterprise system are well enough known that they require no elaboration. I would like to congratulate the writer and publisher of this book on a most commendable undertaking as this nation moves into its third century.

All of my friends, our fans, and most definitely the members of our Musical Family, are well aware of my feelings about the most important ingredient of success—Work!

Having been born and raised on a farm, I have, since childhood, accepted work as naturally as breathing, and to me it has been just about as important to life.

"To earn your bread by the sweat of your brow" is not a myth. It is a cold, hard reality. It applies to all.

Whether we choose to be in the home, office, factory, or field—whether we cook meals, keep books, make automobiles, or sell insurance, the common denominator for success is work.

Without it man loses his vision, his confidence, and his enthusiasm. His life becomes largely meaningless.

On the other hand, there is no other preventative or cure so effective for boredom and fatigue; or for many of our mental and emotional ills, as an honest day's work every working day of the year. There is no limit to the rich things that we may have—material, mental, spiritual—if we work hard enough to obtain them.

Know what you want! Work for it—and the earth will yield its treasures to you.

SECTION

4

ABOUT WARREN T. BROOKES

Warren T. Brookes is a featured columnist for the Boston Herald American, specializing in economic affairs. He describes himself as one who "believes passionately in the free market system and a foe of ever-expanding government control," which he sees as smothering individual freedom in America.

His columns have presented factual and stirring arguments on behalf of those beliefs as applied to vital national issues of the day, such as *inflation, energy, welfare reform, taxation, education, income security, and unemployment.*

He attended Brooks School in North Andover, Massachusetts, and went on to major in economics and marketing at Harvard, graduating Cum Laude in 1952.

In 1976 he won the United Press award for "Outstanding Community Service" for a series on the fiscal problems of Boston. His introduction to THE RIGHT TO BE POSITIVE ABOUT FREEDOM, starting on the following page, was first presented in the Herald American in July, 1977 and has been reprinted in various forms in more than 50 newspapers and magazines, including the "Editor's Page" of U.S. News & World Report, issue of October 17, 1977. It is an eloquent plea for a return to sanity in government.

THE RIGHT TO BE POSITIVE ABOUT FREEDOM

By WARREN T. BROOKES

During the past few years, it has become fashionable in the media, generally, to refer to any politician who votes against major spending programs as "negative" or "lacking in compassion."

Similarly, politicians who regularly vote for vast government social enterprises are regarded as "positive" or "compassionate" and being "for the people" or "liberal."

In this political lexicon, then, any politician who attempts to stand for limited government, and for individual freedom and responsibility, risks being branded as "negative."

To this automatic response we should pose a rather simple question: "What is negative about freedom?"

Or, to put it another way, what is "negative" about preserving the right of individual citizens to live their own lives free of the constant interference of government, and the excessive burden of its taxation?

But then, let's turn it around. What, we may well ask is "positive" or "liberal" about a government that now takes almost 44 percent of the nation's total personal income?

What is "positive" about a government that runs annual deficits of over $50 billion—and prints money to finance them?

What is "positive" about a constant inflation rate of nearly 7 percent—a rate at which half of your life savings are destroyed every 10 or 12 years?

What is "positive" and "liberal" about a government whose regulations now cost consumers more than $100 billion a year?

What is "positive" or "liberal" about a Social Security system that is now taking more from the taxpayers than they can ever get back —and still going bankrupt?

What is "positive" about a public education system that spends over $1500 a year per student—and doesn't teach them how to read, write, or do arithmetic?

What is "positive" about a welfare system that is turning millions of Americans into helpless wards of the state, and encouraging millions of others to choose dependence instead of work?

What is "positive" about a government whose total accumulated long term debt and obligations are over $5 trillion—more than the total worth of the economy?

What is "positive" about more than $4 billion in known welfare abuse, error and fraud?

What is "positive" about a nation where there are nearly 85 full-time dependents or employees of government for every 100 productive private taxpayers?

What is "positive" about a government which is printing money at a rate more than twice as fast as the nation's economy is growing?

What is "positive" or "liberal" about asking government bureaucrats to make decisions for you which you are better able to make for yourself and at much lower cost?

In short, what is "positive" about big government, with all its trappings of bureaucratic power, waste and arrogance, and with all its constant threats to individual freedom, privacy and expression?

We think we know what Thomas Jefferson would have said to these rhetorical questions. In 1801 he wrote: "Every man wishes to pursue his occupation and to enjoy the fruits of his labors and the produce of his property in peace and safety, and with the least possible expense. When these things are accomplished, all the objects for which government ought to be established are answered."

Yet the very "liberal" politicians who regularly hold up Jefferson as their patron saint have, in fact, a very different concept of our government—a concept which, in the name of human security, demands a greater and greater level of government action, spending and domination in every phase of our lives—a concept that in the guise of liberalism, constantly calls for more and more compulsory programs for our individual good and a constant diminution of our freedom.

The reason for all this, of course, is that, far from being "positive" or "liberal", these power-hungry politicians and bureaucrats have a very "negative" and authoritarian view of mankind.

They see us not as independent individuals, able to take care of our own lives, but as helpless collective groups of "little people" with constant needs and problems which only a benevolent government can provide and solve.

They encourage us, not to strive for individual dominion, achievement and reliance, but for the vain and unholy grail of security and protection by an increasingly expensive and expansive central government.

Above all, they seem to forget that it was Jefferson, the philosophical mentor of the American Revolution, who wrote over 170 years ago that:

"If a nation values anything more than freedom, it will lose its freedom—and the irony of it is that if it is comfort or money that it values more than freedom, it will lose the comfort and the money too."

As this nation moves into its third century of independence and ponders immense and far-reaching decisions about the direction of its government and its society, we would do well to ask ourselves again the question: WHAT IS NEGATIVE ABOUT FREEDOM?

Warren T. Brookes

What's Washington got, that you haven't got? Your money

GOVERNMENTS want you to think they have magic words, special abilities, genius you can't match or understand — they can do big things for you.

With what? Government makes no money, produces nothing, has not a dime it doesn't take from you, out of your profits or your income.

And governments are just people — people like you and me — and some of them not as good.

But you have hired them to spend the money you give them. See that they spend it for the greatest good of the nation — *your* good, not theirs.

It's your money. Never forget it.

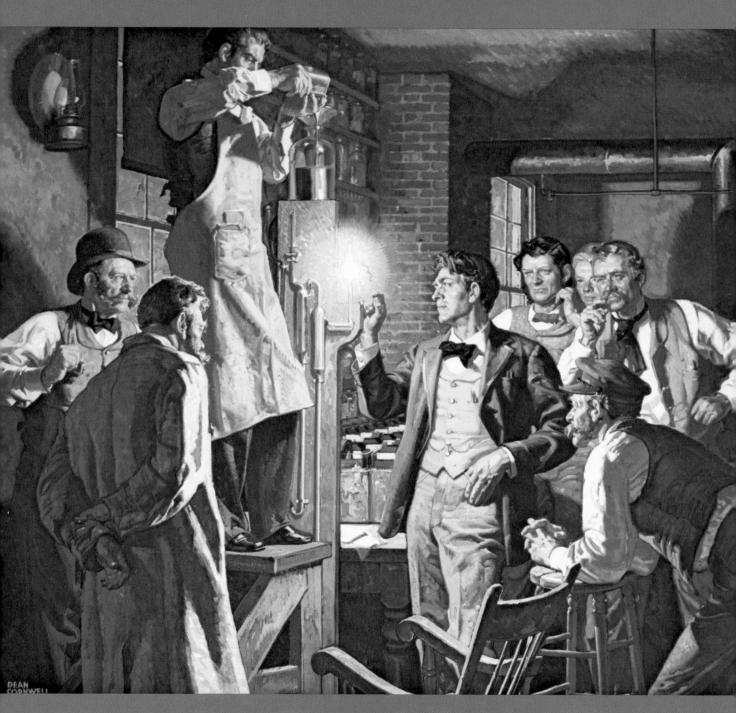

From painting of Thomas Edison and his associates
contemplating for forty hours, his first successful
incandescent bulb.

Courtesy of General Electric's Lamp Business
Division.

What's free about Free Enterprise?

— double the light and power for every penny you spend for electricity.

— 15,000 added miles in an automobile tire.

— clothing that lasts longer, looks better, launders more easily.

— safer, more convenient home refrigeration at a fraction the cost of the old-fashioned method.

— orange juice in cans the year 'round, instead of oranges only during short seasons.

— lawn mowers you don't have to push.

— new plastics, better metals, synthetic fabrics which make hundreds of things last longer.

— yes, and years added to many lives, by modern drugs developed by enterprising drug companies.

Incentive? The search for profit, which spurred these and a thousand other improvements — and in the process created millions more jobs.

So hadn't we better look with a hard cold eye at the many people who are trying so hard (and too successfully) to attack profit and take the *freedom* out of free enterprise?

The most successful freedom march was the one in covered wagons

THAT, too, was made by Americans — looking for work. No demands, no subsidies, no claim anyone owed them anything. They traveled mostly on foot and through deadly danger, to where there was work to do (they didn't ask it be brought to them nor created for them).

Many had never been prosperous — their little farms were worked out, or their skills weren't very good. But their self-respect was real enough to drive them through thousands of miles of unspeakable hardship, and there create their own jobs and their own futures.

And that courage and self-respect and hard work were what made America's splendid West.

If there were more White Jackets in this country it would be a better country

IF you ever attend a Homecoming at the College of William and Mary, you'll see a famous Governor, or a College President, perhaps a prominent editor, famous doctors, lawyers, bankers, business executives, ministers, civic leaders — all proudly wearing white jackets. That signifies these men earned all or most of their way through college, waiting on table.

They weren't ashamed of menial labor, they didn't hold out for the job they liked, they didn't ask for government help — they *waited on table,* and it helped them earn the education they have since put to such splendid use.

The Order of the White Jacket has a roster of which any college club or fraternity or group of any kind in the land could well be proud. There ought to be a chapter of this magnificent organization on every college campus in America.

Contributing alumni of all schools please note.

"The time is very short, and the choice is very clear. Either we preserve the vitality of this great free enterprise system — our way of life — or we face children some day when they will ask us where we were, and what we were doing, on the day that freedom was lost."

— Ronald Reagan

SECTION

5

ABOUT PHILIP M. CRANE

Phil Crane, member of Congress from Illinois, is a brilliant intellectual (one of only 16 members with a Ph.D. degree) who has been battling the reckless spenders in Congress since first elected in 1969— the last time by 75 percent of the vote.

His educational credentials are more than impressive: Hillsdale College in Michigan; DePauw University, Indiana; University of Michigan; University of Vienna; M.A. and Ph.D. degrees from Indiana University, teaching history at the latter for three years.

When so many others gloomingly surrender to the argument that the federal budget cannot be balanced because most spending has been man-

dated by law, his instant retort is: "Nonsense. The Congress has mandated every expenditure and what Congress can do, it can also undo."

In his scholarly book, *The Sum of Good Government*, which he calls a labor of love, he finishes on an optimistic note: "It is not too late to turn things around," citing the many growing pressures and disenchantment of the people with big government, spending their country into bankruptcy.

Author of a detailed study and proposal on how to cut the federal budget by $53 billion, he is one of the most forceful and articulate members of congress, fighting for a free and solvent America.

THE RIGHT TO HOLD OUR LAWMAKERS ACCOUNTABLE FOR THE RAVAGES OF INFLATION.

Robbing the young, impoverishing the old, and eroding the liberties of all.

By U.S. REP. PHILIP M. CRANE

Inflation is like a little dope—there is no such thing. It becomes an acid eating a bigger and bigger hole in your pocket, and like the sand in an hour glass, it is only a matter of time when your pocket is empty—or, what may be left in it will be worthless.

All economic theories aside, the brunt of the blame falls squarely on the shoulders of Congress. For it is these elected representatives who continue to approve boondoggle spending programs—$40, $50, $60 billion a year beyond the Treasury's income—thus making necessary deficit borrowing which, in turn, sets off the deadly inflationary spiral.

Surprising as it may seem today, the federal budget only exceeded $1 billion once before 1917 and stood at $9 billion as late as 1940. The $100 billion mark was not reached until 1962, but from there it took us only nine more years to reach $200 billion, another four years to hit $300 billion, and only two more to surpass $400 billion. At this rate, federal spending could reach $1 trillion by the mid 1980's! All of this would not be so devastating if the nation's economy permitted collecting the taxes to pay for it. But it does not, and the result is a gargantuan national deficit and a skyrocketing national debt.

The same growth can be seen in that national debt. In 1930 it was only $15.9 billion. Just thirty years later it was $286.1 billion, and by the end of 1976 it was $576.6 billion. For 1977 the Congress gave the nod to a "temporary" debt ceiling figure of $752 billion!

If this trend continues, the national debt should hit the $1 trillion mark by 1980. Interest alone on such a debt would be roughly $85 billion, or 85% as much as our current budget for national defense. One must ask, **at what point will interest obligations exceed our ability to meet them and thus bring national bankruptcy through default of servicing the national debt?**

Let me illustrate the undeniable relationship between deficit spending and inflation. From December 31, 1957, to December 31, 1975, the national debt increased from $334.7 billion to $516.6 billion—an increase of 67.6 per cent. During the same period the cost of living index increased a remarkably similar 63.7%! Those figures are not just coincidental; **they are proof that deficit spending is the prime cause of inflation.**

Further, inflation is a cruel means of hiding so-called unseen taxes. Not only do budget deficits cause more money to chase a relatively fixed amount of goods, thus driving up consumer prices and diminishing the purchasing power of your money, but even those lucky enough to secure wage increases pegged to the cost of living find themselves owing more tax dollars as they move into a higher tax bracket.

But the real sufferers are the many millions of Americans with fixed incomes whose standard of living must go down, down, down —year after year, after year; losing homes, eating less, neglecting health care, and fearing they will live too long.

Of course Congress has a cute gimmick by which it protects itself from the increased cost of living. It simply votes itself a pay raise and sends you the bill. Instead of owning up to fiscal irresponsibility which has jacked up the cost of living, Congress compensates itself as if for a job well done.

Another grizzly fact is the inflationary pressures from abroad that our current state of energy dependence on foreign sources exerts. When Congress refuses to let the free market operate in the energy domain, and instead approves a tax bill designed to cut the energy industry off from investment capital that would accrue from expected higher prices, we are even more under the Arabs heel, and we still pay the higher prices. By denying U.S. firms the capacity to develop alternate domestic supplies, the House has assured the American people that an increase in OPEC oil will be transferred directly into increased prices at home. It almost seems as if the Democratic majority in Congress would rather give money to the Arabs than to grant American oil firms a chance to prosper and create more American jobs. Hopefully, by publication date of this book, the Senate will have corrected this mess.

Attitude is the key. There is a gap of billions of dollars between Congress spending as much as it can for social programs and special interest schemes vs. their having the integrity and character to spend only what is vitally necessary until we can afford to do more. That difference could mean a balanced budget and the end of inflation.

In short, the buck stops here—in the House and in the Senate. But it will only stop when the public rises in its wrath to make itself heard. Believe me, Congressmen listen when the people back home make themselves heard and demand a full explanation of voting records that spell inflation.

For Congress is the ultimate determiner of spending policy. If it has the power to create an unbalanced budget, it also has the power to give us a balanced budget. Those so-called "uncontrollables" in the budget process are "uncontrollable" only because Congress has made them so. And what Congress can do, it can also undo. All that is necessary is a sense of fiscal responsibility and the will-power to act upon it. And the source of that will power? YOU, the people who put them there and who possess the power to send them home if they do not act with accountability to preserve your savings and your security.

And now, read on. The messages which follow are filled with hope.

Phil Crane

Who cares about inflation— until dinner-time?

MORE money for everything you sell or make, more money for every hour you work... what's wrong with that?

Only that we all *buy* as well as sell, so—when you get more per hour for making bread but don't bake more loaves, the price I pay for bread has to go up, to pay your increase. And when I get more for raising a steer, you pay more for eating steak. Neither one of us is any better off, and the millions on pensions or any sort of fixed income are all worse off—they just don't eat as much bread or steak or anything else. Their income increases (if any) *creep* upward, while the prices they have to pay *leap* up. That's why inflation unless it is stopped leads to collapse.

Inflation is greed—getting more than you give, demanding more than you earn. *Everybody* suffers.

Scene in the House of Representatives. A witticism
from the chair. Wash drawing by Arthur I. Keller

Who's wearing the mask in this biggest robbery in history?

A MILLION dollar robbery rightly stirs public wrath and the demand the money be found and the culprits be punished. Yet Americans with savings in banks and in life insurance were robbed of 60 *billion* dollars last year because of inflation — 60 billion dollars which does no one any good, which can never provide capital for new businesses and new jobs, 60 billion which can never assure independence for the old people who saved it, 60 billion which can never build homes for young people, nor gifts to schools and hospitals — 60 evaporated *billions.*

Who's to blame? All governments, Federal and local, who spend more than they take in; all agencies who waste your money on boondoggling and vote-getting; all bureaus more interested in saving their jobs than in saving this country's solvency. *And every American* who wants more then he is willing to produce and pay for.

Instead of writing your government to *give* you something, write them to *save* it.

Source of amount (see above) — American Institute for Economic Research

Are we telling our children the truth about what we're leaving them?

THE recklessly planted seeds of inflation that grow and wipe out savings, insurance, bonds, pensions, security. Whenever the government spends a single dollar more than it takes in, that is another seed of poisonous inflation.

The brain-numbing habit of looking to government for "security"—destroying the self-reliance that built America and without which this nation cannot survive.

The encouragement of pressure groups to "get theirs" at the expense of the nation, by threatening elected officials with defeat unless they truckle to those militant minorities.

Not such a wonderful legacy to leave your children, is it? If *parents* would recapture self-respect by *self-reliance* for a change, there might still be some of *America* left in the estate you leave.

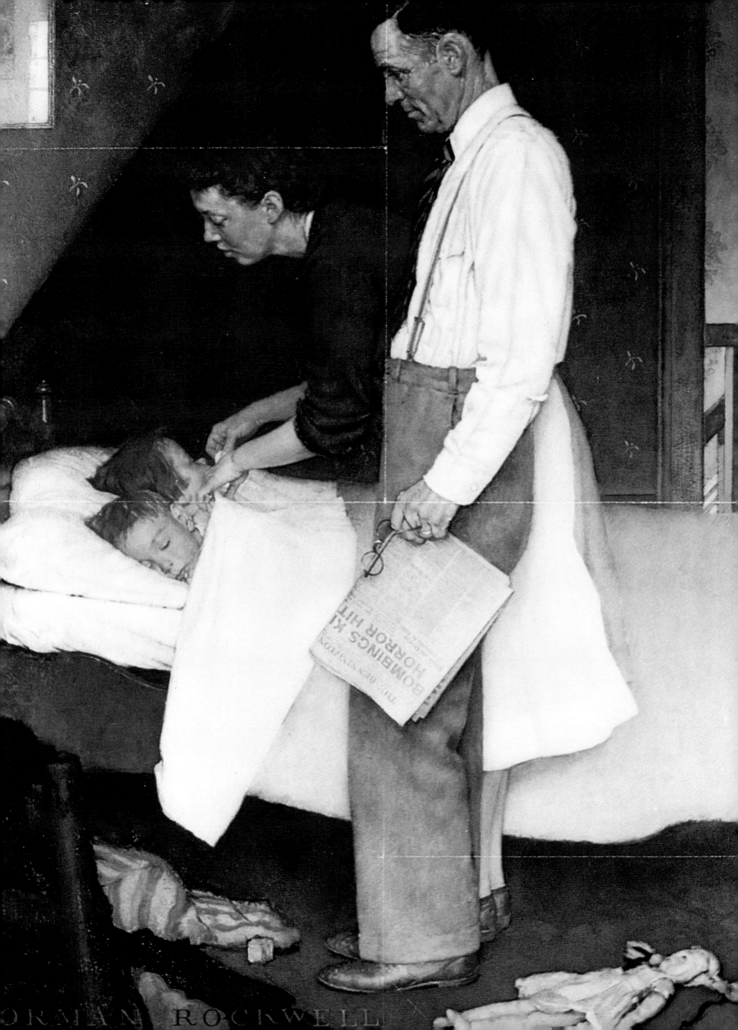

Tighten your belt,
not your noose

IF WE would all *demand* sacrificing some luxuries which some people say are important but aren't — if we'd cut out deficit spending and printing paper money to "pay" for it — we'd throw off the noose of inflation that is strangling this nation.

If we had more confidence in a hard-work future than a dole-for-votes present, there would be a glorious American future and it could start now.

"When, oh when, will we learn that, as a people, we cannot receive more than we contribute?"

Howard K. Smith
A.B.C. news cast.

Pampered Pets

ALMOST every city, county, state in the nation has its pet project that it "simply cannot get along without," and the nation itself has scores if not hundreds:

... such as the southern city which *must* have a scenic waterfront boulevard (half paid for by Federal funds). Why? It has got along very well without it for a hundred years. Couldn't they just postpone it until the country is financially healthy again?

... or the town which *has* to have three new school buildings, when cleaning up the old ones (and punishing vandalism in them) could do for a while, anyway.

... *more* Federal employees, when many of the millions we already have aren't earning their keep.

... junkets by congressmen "to see about conditions in this or that part of the world." Couldn't our embassies and consuls already there and familiar with local facts find out for them?

It all comes out of the heavy laden taxpayer.

Thinking men and women are frightened by the deadly results of inflation. And a major cause of inflation is spending more than we take in and printing money to pay for the resulting deficits.

Memo to Washington:

You'd be surprised what most of us do without (You ought to try it, sometime)

A high government official didn't like the blue carpet in his new office, so he ordered a new gold carpet costing taxpayers $48,000.

The National Science Foundation is spending $84,000 to find out why people fall in love.

We work in a perfectly decent office building, but our boss doesn't provide each of us with a suite including kitchenette and lavatory — as many Government officials provide for themselves.

The FTC spent 18 days in which 20 witnesses filled 1700 pages of testimony against a manufacturer who dared to advertise his soft drink as "sensible" and "high in vitamin C." The FTC judge then threw out the charges.

We understand the Defense Department produced 12 separate films showing soldiers and sailors how to brush their teeth.

While industry is forced to lay off thousands of important, productive workers, government for years has hired an average of 1200 people *per day*.

This sorry tale could go on page after page, but you get the idea, Washington, don't you?

We *hope* so.

Government cannot make men prosperous any more than it can make men good. Government cannot produce anything. It can merely seize and divide up what individuals produce. Government can give the people nothing which government has not first taken away from them. And the amount which government doles back to the people or spends to promote their welfare is always less than what it takes, because of the excessive costs of governmental administration.

—Dan Smoot

SECTION

6

ABOUT JOSEPH T. BAILEY

Joseph T. Bailey is Chairman and Chief Executive Officer of the world-wide, century-old Warner & Swasey Company, leaders in the machine tool industry and headquartered in Cleveland, Ohio.

After 25 years in general management positions with General Electric Company, he joined Warner & Swasey as Director of Research and Development and was rapidly promoted to division general manager, group vice-president, executive vice-president and president. He was appointed Chairman in 1973.

Congenial and down-to-earth, Bailey is a fervent defender of American free enterprise. Under his leadership, the Warner & Swasey editorial advertising series has continued its

forty-two year campaign to heal the American spirit and expose the perils to liberty inherent in uncontrolled government spending beyond the people's ability to pay.

Joe Bailey is a scholarly economic realist, as well as a working humanitarian—a leader in civic and charitable activities in Cleveland. He points out that if private business was run like the federal government, it would be bankrupt before it opened its doors. He is driven by a passionate need to warn his fellow Americans of just such a fate for their government if the people do not demand that it change its ways.

His message which follows should be absorbed by every citizen before stepping into the voting booth.

THE RIGHT TO TAKE ACTION AGAINST THE PERILS OF GOVERNMENT SPENDING BEYOND THE PEOPLE'S ABILITY TO PAY

By JOSEPH T. BAILEY

I often wonder if the founding fathers of the United States of America had any idea how distant and impersonal the government they designed would become. I wonder if they realized how little influence the American people would have on the decisions of their government. I wonder if they could have predicted the waste and inefficiency of federal, state and local governments or the incredible appetites they would develop. I wonder if they could have envisioned the behavior of the American people today—a people who have suffered high taxes, erosion of their income and savings through inflation, regulation of virtually every aspect of their lives and, worst of all, most having meekly accepted it.

The battle cry of "No taxation without representation!" was a stirring protest by colonial America. Yet today, with full representation, fewer than half of eligible voters turn out for most national elections. And of those who do vote, the great majority are uninformed as to whom or what they are voting for. Is it any wonder we have elected representatives who squander our nation's wealth?

The British economic oppression that led to the American Revolution was mild in comparison to the economic oppression of "big government" today. It is astounding to realize that taxes now consume more than 40% of the citizen's income. In contrast, the British in 1776 imposed no taxes on colonial income, only taxes on goods, and these amounted to far less than the sales taxes alone, levied by state governments today.

We are in an age of "big government," expensive government. How big is big? Consider the fact that America now has more government workers than direct production workers!

These government workers produce no goods. Government is a consumer. Its growth is fed by increased taxes—taxes on the people and business which produce all the wealth in America. Its growth is further fed by deficit spending, a ruinous course that has led to a spiral of inflation and still higher taxes.

The "big government" we now support has produced a national debt three-and-one-half times the amount of the collected savings of all Americans! It is so large that it now takes all of the income taxes paid by two-thirds of all Americans just to pay the interest on the debt! And the debt keeps growing—for instance forty billion dollars a year—the cost for forms and reports that bureaucrats have dreamed up and then stored away in more costly government buildings.

These figures represent only what our government owes today. Current estimates by the National Taxpayers Union place our future commitments at a debt of $5,700,000,000,000. That's 5.7 trillion dollars! To give that number a meaning, the Commerce Clearing House estimates that 5.7 trillion dollars represents the total value of all property in America—including automobiles, houses, factories, offices, wrist watches, everything. In other words, everything we possess is in hock.

Now there is no way under the sun that a debt of that magnitude can ever be repaid. To put it in perspective, 5.7 trillion breaks down to $108,000 per family.

Is there any doubt that on its present course, our government is headed for bankruptcy?

Why has this happened? Any businessman can provide that answer. It has happened because government has operated without restraint. It has been allowed to create "funny money"—money that is not backed by anything of real value—only by government's promise to repay.

In business, funny money is not allowed. A business cannot borrow money unless it has sufficient assets to repay the debt. Those assets are measured in terms of real value—property, equipment, cash on hand, inventory and accounts receivable. A promise to repay is of no value to a lending institution. A loan must be backed or it is not given.

An individual's credit is limited by the same sensible policy. A person who borrows money to buy a car cannot borrow more than the car is worth. And in most cases, a cash down payment is needed, so that the loan is actually for less than the car is worth. Meanwhile, the bank or finance company retains title to the car as collateral. If the debt is not promptly or fully paid, the car is repossessed.

For businesses and individuals, this is how restraint operates on spending. For government, a different set of rules seem to apply.

Who is responsible for placing proper restraints on government? Voters are responsible, because votes determine who will run government. And the people who run government control the purse strings of America.

Unfortunately, the vote has not proved to be the powerful tool that America's founders thought it would be. Politicians recognize that. They get elected by promising more, more, more. And the American people go along without realizing that more, more, more yields less, less, less. More government spending means more taxes, higher inflation and less spendable income for Americans.

This section of "The Rebirth of a Nation" addresses the *right* of the people to take action against government overspending. I believe it is now more than a *right* because the past has shown that this is a *right* that has not been exercised. The results are witnessed in the deteriorating financial condition of America, in high taxes and inflation. That *right* has now become an obligation, and unless the American people move to accept their obligation, the bankruptcy of America cannot be far away. Senator Goldwater, in his book, THE COMING BREAK-POINT, gives us less than ten years at the present rate of irresponsible governing of America from Washington.

As the National Taxpayers Union points out: "Few people realize how much influence ordinary taxpayers can have over government policies. Our political system responds to pressure. That is why the beneficiaries of government spending have been able to receive tremendous windfalls at your expense. They have been well organized and have applied pressure in the right places.

"If you want to help persuade Congress to start balancing federal budgets, all you have to do is say so. And it will only cost you 13¢—the cost of sending a letter direct to your representative in Washington. Politicians respond to numbers, not logic. It is volume that counts. Congressmen know that each person who bothers to send a letter represents thousands of voters."

A "Rebirth of our Nation" will come when the people take back their country and see that it is run like they run their own lives—with prudence, integrity and doing without what they cannot pay for.

So what can voters do? The answer is summed up in a 1975 Warner & Swasey editorial titled, "WRITE YOUR CONGRESSMAN and tell him what *not* to do for you, what *not* to give you. Tell him all you want is a solvent America which lives within its income, *whatever* that may be. Make sure he knows you mean it. And tell him there isn't much time left."

J. T. Bailey

It wasn't the Goths that defeated Rome—It was the free circuses

LUXURIES, power, indulgence had made the once-tough Roman people soft. To stay popular, their emperors gave them more and more of the ease they craved—free bread, free circuses, easier living.

So the Romans softened up themselves for the ambitious, hard-working barbarians. And in 410 A.D. the greatest nation the world had ever seen was invaded and destroyed.

The greedy cry of "something for nothing," the stupid whine of "somebody else should sacrifice, not me"—could do *exactly the same for this nation*, NOW.

"Pass me another chocolate cream; I've raised my weight limit again"

ANYONE flirting with a heart attack from overweight, but who quiets his conscience by saying higher and higher weights are safe, would be declared insane.

Then what do you call a government which insists it is solvent since it "is within the legal debt limit," and whenever it wants to spend or waste more money simply votes a raise in that "legal limit!"

And like the man who "rigs" the scales so his true weight won't all show, that government doesn't count many fixed obligations which would almost double that debt.

Who's kidding whom?

"NONSENSE! IF IT GETS TOO DEEP, YOU CAN EASILY PULL ME OUT!"

Where does "Federal aid" come from?

THESE new roads, schools, harbors, post offices, bureaucrats, pensions, government aid won't cost you anything — it's "*Federal* money."

And where does Federal money come from? YOU. The government has nothing except what it collects from you. And a lot of what it collects is wasted in the costs of collection. You'd be far better off if you paid for your own "benefits" direct.

Of course there *is* one other place the government can get money — by printing it. But that makes savings accounts, bonds, pensions, life insurance worth less and less; print enough and they're worth nothing.

So next time some politician promises you something for nothing, remember it's *your* money he's giving to somebody else. Treat him the way *that* deserves.

The Federal Aid that's really needed is aid to the taxpayer

FOR forty years the American taxpayer has been pouring out his hard-earned dollars all over his own country and the world.

The typical American is taught from childhood that you work or starve; your only security is to spend less than you earn; no one owes you anything — you use your own money for pleasure, or save it for security, or give it to deserving causes as you please.

But now kindness has been replaced in too many places by pressures . . . "Pay me what I want or I'll go communist," and people too improvident to provide for themselves by self-denial expect you to pay their bills by *your* self-denial.

The American taxpayer, who pays all these bills is being taxed at a higher rate than most of the people he benefits. Experts say we are near, and may have passed, the point where taxes kill American ambition without which there can be no progress nor growth.

The plain, unhappy truth is that the goose that lays the world's golden egg is being worked to death.

"I predict future happiness for Americans if they can prevent the government from wasting the labors of the people under the pretense of taking care of them."

— Thomas Jefferson

Instead of meekly paying more taxes we'd better demand less spending

HOW long are you going to put up with having your taxes double in ten years? That is what they have done — and will keep on doing , as long as you permit your Federal, State and Local governments to spend *750 billion dollars* a year (up 11% from the year before) *up* year after year after year.

Estimated taxes are $8050 per American household!

The cure is simple and sure — *cut spending,* especially for those pet projects whose objective is votes. There are too many government employees. There are too many government bureaus. There are too many government programs.

Bitter resistance against excessive taxes is long overdue. If you agree, let's say so. *Loud and clear.*

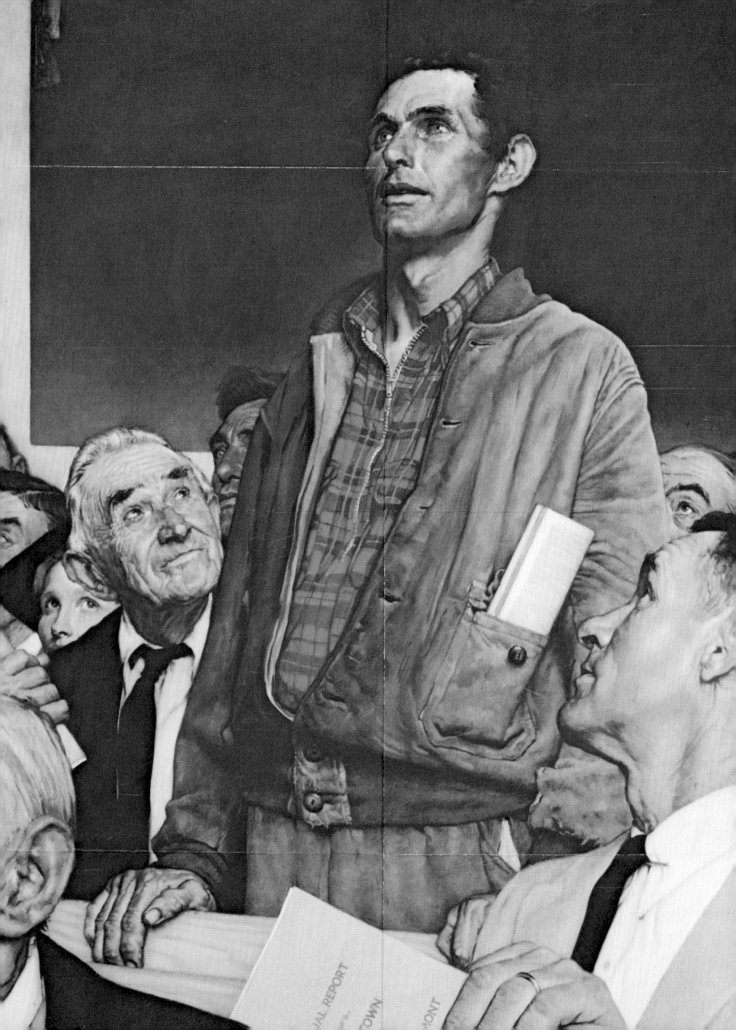

You can't bribe poverty to go away—you have to work it to death

RELIEF may keep body and soul together but it's hard on the soul. If relief were restricted to the truly helpless—if waste and dishonesty were cut out of the program and this money used instead to teach men and women to work and produce for themselves—then we would be on the way at last to the truly honest, compassionate plan for which Relief was originally designed.

Almost all people can be taught to produce something useful. And they should, because the simplest ability honestly applied can lead to skill, and skill can lead to self-reliance and self-respect—and happiness. And that, after all, is what it's all about.

You can't vote yourself security—you earn it

LET'S be honest with ourselves—in this troubled world there *is* no such thing as *security* any more. (Even the dictionary says the definition of secure as "confident" is "archaic.")

You eat and wear and are sheltered by what you have produced. Therefore, the more you produce (and don't squander) the more you can save, and the more secure you are.

Everything within reason which makes it impossible for you and me to save should be corrected. And that includes unions who restrict production and therefore workers' savings, governments who waste and therefore tax away savings, businessmen who refuse their workers the means of better production and therefore greater savings.

There will always be some indigent, sick or old who cannot produce; they must be taken care of by the rest of us, of course. But that is charity, which is right, not security which is not *a* right but is our own individual doing, earned by hard work.

"WORKING HANDS"
Woodcut by M. Welman

"When shallow critics denounce the profit motive inherent in our system of private enterprise, they ignore the fact that this is the economic support of every right we possess, and that without it, all rights would soon disappear. Their conclusions emphasize the results: more and more bureaus, more and more taxes, fewer and fewer producers, and finally financial collapse and the end of freedom.

— Dwight D. Eisenhower

Who does the most for the country?

(Who profits most from profit?)

DID the Liberals save millions of American women from back-breaking work by inventing the vacuum cleaner and washing machine — or was it businessmen looking for profit?

Did union leaders create modern life-giving drugs, or was it businesses in search of profit?

Is it government bureaucracy or profit-seeking corporations which generate the millions of American jobs paying the highest wages in the world?

Was it the Welfare State or men who wanted to become millionaires who developed the automobile and the hundreds of thousands of jobs which followed?

When those who criticize and attack profit can equal this record for their country, it will be time to listen to them.

But not until.

GENTLEMEM
OUR
COUNTRY

HENRY FORD. AND HIS FIRST CAR.

Photograph courtesy of Ford Motor Co. Museum.

"Redistributing the wealth" = sharing the poverty

A farmer has two fields — one rocky and barren, one of rich black loam.

Does he dig up the rich loam and scatter it over the rocks? That is "redistributing the wealth," which our social reformers demand. Same thing as Marx's idea: "From each according to his abilities; to each according to his needs."

But only a fool for a farmer would do that, because then he'd have two poor fields, and no good one.

The wise farmer (and wise reformer and labor leader and Government official) lets the rich field grow and prosper and produce; and he plows and fertilizes and limes and works the poor field until it produces, too.

Then the farmer has two good fields from which everyone benefits — instead of two poor fields, with which everyone starves.

Some of our "tax experts" might take a look at Nature. She seems to have the answers — and in *Nature* they *work*.

"The forging of America, as the greatest success story in history, was no accident. It was the direct result of our marvelous free enterprise system."

—Jack F. Kemp
Member of Congress, New York

Measuring big government by the magnitude of a billion:

   1 billion seconds ago — the bombing of Pearl Harbor.

   1 billion minutes ago — Christ was living on earth.

   1 billion hours ago — man had not yet appeared on earth, but...

   1 billion dollars ago — that was only yesterday.

— Quoted in "The Farmer Stockman of the Midwest."

SECTION

7

ABOUT JAMES BROWNING ALLEN

1912-1978

(Excerpted from Eulogy by U.S. Senator
Harry F. Byrd, Jr. June 6, 1978)

Through the years, just as it does now, the Senate
of the United States has had within its membership
so many splendid and outstanding individuals. But
never have I known a finer man than James B. Allen,
nor one in whom I have had greater confidence.

What a combination of qualities did the Alabama
Senator possess—strong convictions, great courage
and a fierce determination to protect the principles
of government in which he deeply believed.

Yet, with it all, he was kind and thoughtful and
humble.

If what Jefferson called the "inalienable rights" of
the minority are safeguarded, there must be
sentinels of democracy, vigorous champions of
those who may hold views contrary to the passing
but powerful majorities of the day. Such a sentinel,
such a champion, was Senator James B. Allen of
Alabama . . . his fairness and integrity became a
legend in the Senate . . . a legend based on the un-
assailable fact that James Allen was a man whose
dedication and courage were matched only by his
honesty and sense of justice.

He was, indeed, a servant of the people, giving,
without limit, his time and talent—and sacrificing
his health.

In his death, the people of Alabama have lost an
unselfish and dedicated champion; the Senate of the
United States has lost a courageous and, perhaps,
irreplaceable leader, and I have lost a dear friend.

THE RIGHT TO CHOOSE LIBERTY AND SELF ACHIEVEMENT OVER THE CHAINS OF THE WELFARE STATE.

By U.S. SENATOR JAMES B. ALLEN
(Written Just Prior To His Demise, June 1, 1978)

So Far Have We Gone Astray

The social engineers in Washington seem to think that Americans no longer have the self-mastery to build their lives independent of government nourishment, regulation and direction at every turn. They act as though we are unfit for the liberty of self-dependence and that the great "white father" must intervene and decide what is best for us.

Well, let me say right now, it was individual pride of achievement that created this great nation. The miracle of America was forged when men's dreams put on work clothes and the pioneers set forth armed only with self-esteem, ambition and resolve to compete and excel on their own.

I firmly believe that, in determining his own destiny, every citizen, however humble, has greater wisdom than any government, however great.

Edward Gibbon wrote about the ancient Athenians: "They wanted a comfortable life and they lost it all—security, comfort and freedom. When they finally wanted not to give to society, but for society to give to them; when the freedom they worked for was freedom from responsibility, Athens ceased to be free and was never free again." They learned that when the people failed to exercise their control over government, public servants turned into public masters.

The question is: when does a welfare state destroy the free society that established it? For, it is the sober truth that, as long as government cares for the people, the people will not care for themselves. In a nutshell that is the heart of the problem. It is the tragedy of Great Britain. These great people are learning that nothing is free; that socialism pulls no one up, but drags everyone down; that it is a pestilence leading to a graveyard where freedom is buried.

We, in America, are beginning to learn that social ills cannot be cured with money. If that is all it took there wouldn't be a single poor neighborhood. Washington has been pouring out money by the tens and scores of billions. But that is like trying to cure a painful ailment with morphine. It helps lull the pain for a little while, but then it is back again, and worse, because addiction has been added to the disease.

We cannot legislate equality; we have to deserve it. We cannot demand success; we have to earn it. We cannot be handed an education or skill; we have to learn by hard work. We cannot vote ourselves security; we have to produce and save for it.

How It Began

America's colonization was begun by men and women who believed this. Seeking a new and independent way of life for themselves, they created a society that, in time, was free from the economic, political and religious chains of the Old World. The independent spirit of these settlers was sharpened by their dependence on their own self-reliance to house, feed and protect their families.

And so the country grew, a people jealous of their freedoms, independence, and with pride in their material achievements. They had turned their God-given resources into magnificent cities and great factories and they had an agricultural system that served themselves and had begun to provide sustenance to less developed areas of the world.

How It All Happened

But the price of American progress did not come cheaply. As the factories grew, as the Nation entered the world political arena and brought its vast resources to bear against tyranny abroad, as the great inventions and scientific achievements provided more and more material gains, the institutional framework which had served so well for so long was strained. And, in attempting to accommodate the changes required by progress, our laws and the basis for them underwent significant philosophical modifications.

Statism, collectivism or welfarism are part of any government system to some degree, but in our country these concepts were not translated into statute and public policy until the economic emergency of the 1930's. Then, throughout the Nation, people were overwhelmed by their inability to cope or comprehend their place in the scheme of things. As a result, citizens turned to the promises of those who had political power; for only those, it was assumed, had the power to control the forces in society with economic power. In turning to politics to solve great social problems, the people unknowingly brought upon themselves a substantive change in their system of government which, to this day, threatens to move us in the direction of some type of totalitarianism.

It is no wonder, then, that many Americans believe that government owes them a living, or that health care, housing, welfare, recreational opportunities, retirement security or education are the sole responsibility of the rest of the tax-paying population. Is it any wonder that, as the trend continues, and as generations of Americans accept this "security first" compact, the structure of the American family declines? But, when government has all the power to solve problems, and does not do so, is it any wonder that Americans appear to be disillusioned with their government?

The question is not how to return to simpler times, but rather how to recapture a value system which places the individual at the core of our society and relegates government to its proper role as guardian of rights not the giver of rights.

Welfarism and collectivism will not simply wither away, for there is a reluctance among too many people to accept responsibility which, in turn, means "someone else" must make decisions. That "someone else" leaves the door open for the experimenters, the social-science quacks and charismatic charlatans to manage one's life by government action through added and enlarged social experiments and programs.

The Pendulum Swings

But, I detect a healthy skepticism in the country among people who understand that those others, whether they be government bureaucrats, business magnates, union leaders or whoever, do not know what is best for everyone else. This growing body of opinion offers us the best hope for a safe and individ-

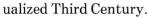

ualized Third Century.

If each of us will accept the role of sacrificing political promises for liberty, we will have taken a giant step toward restructuring the society away from the welfare state. The thinking citizen will not be emboldened to ask for the impossible from his elected representatives—a balanced budget, a stable economy, more "free" benefits and less taxation. He will know, intrinsically, that one cannot have his cake and eat it too.

The automatic fallout from this awareness is that we will begin to ask less of our neighbors. We will be willing to forego public luxuries in order that we might have private freedom. By making this decision, it is axiomatic that we will reinvigorate the work ethic; we will be willing to rely on the profit, free enterprise, capitalist system that provides, not only jobs, but nearly all of our needs.

We will recognize that the most important function of the national government is to protect the society as a whole from foreign aggression and from subversion, injustice and crime at home, and we will gladly pay for such protection.

Beyond that, the aware citizen will question, probe, analyze and, in many cases, reject promises of programs by special interest groups that will cost him more of the fruits of his productive labors. If we are to stop the drift toward welfarism and bring about a "Rebirth of our Nation" these decisions provide the key.

The place to start is with a sense of fiscal responsibility. Another way of saying it is that we, the people, must begin to curb the appetites of those who would do for others, with someone else's money, that which they would refuse to do with their own. This is the essence of moderation and temperance, and a virtue in itself. It could be the means of keeping the welfare state from engulfing an otherwise free people.

The messages which follow lend emphasis to these beliefs.

James B. Allen

The Communist ideology is to destroy your society. That has been their aim for 125 years and has never changed; only the methods have changed... the primary, the eternal concept is humanity. And communism is anti-humanity.

Do we really have to wait for the moment when the knife is at our throats? Couldn't it be possible, ahead of time, soberly to assess the world-wide menace that threatens to swallow the whole world? I was swallowed myself. I have been in the dragon's belly, in the red burning belly of the dragon. He wasn't able to digest me. He threw me up. I have come to you as a witness to what it's like there, in the dragon's belly.

—ALEXANDER SOLZHENITSYN
Speech to AFL-CIO July 9, 1975

If the lion and the lamb
are going to lie down together,
I want to be the lion.
Don't you?

Why do they
want to come
to America?

MILLIONS of men and women, in every country in Europe and Asia, would sell their souls for the chance to live in America. They have experienced workers' governments, socialism, government ownership, communism, fascism, governments run "for the people," countries where land and wealth are confiscated and given to the people. They have experienced all these "Utopias" — and they are frantic to leave them and come to America with its profit system, its corporations, its opportunity for the man willing to work hard.

These people aren't schoolroom theorists; they know from bitter, galling experience that life, liberty, enough to eat, and the right to pursue happiness are possible *only* under the American method of private capital investment in the tools of production, which over the years steadily increases *real* wages — the American system where every man is responsible for his own welfare and too proud to let a government assume that responsibility for him.

To much of that American system has been whittled away these past years. We'd better get it back before it's too late!

*"America lies in the heart of every man
everywhere who hopes to find a land
where he will be free to work out his own
destiny as he chooses."*
— Woodrow Wilson

HARVESTING IN RUSSIA

If Russia bought our system they wouldn't have to buy our grain.

IN RUSSIA 36 million workers were necessary on Russian farms, and they still had to buy millions of tons of our wheat and corn. In America one farmer raises food enough for himself and 42 others — only 5 million farm workers are needed here.

In China one farmer feeds only himself and one other.

In Italy one in 6 has to be on farms. In France, one in 7.

You'd think more countries would discover that it's savings, investment, production machinery and above all, the *opportunity for profit* that feeds the world and always will — if left alone.

Heavy the oar to him who is tired,
Heavy the coat, heavy the sea.

"If I don't go, I don't get"

IN THE South is an old man with a rowboat who ferries passengers across a mile-wide river for 10 cents.

Asked, "How many times a day do you do this?" he said, "As many times as I can because the more I go, the more I get. *And if I don't go, I don't get.*"

That's all you need to know — all there *is* to know — about business, economics, prosperity — *and self-respect.*

"Old Blind Tom" never took a nickel of
welfare in his life. Although blind, he
"made it" on his own selling notions on
the streets of Joplin, Missouri, for 40
years. He died in 1970.

Oil on canvass by Charles Veteto

Washing dishes isn't demeaning: refusing the job, to stay on relief IS

THERE isn't a single honest job that is beneath the dignity of any man with self-respect. You would be surprised at the thousands of successful men who started at any job, at any pay they could get. In our own Company some of our best machinists started here as sweepers.

But the man who refuses a job, using the excuse that it is beneath him, demeans himself because he is proclaiming that he would rather live off the charity of men who work than carry his share.

Landing of the Pilgrims at Plymouth Rock, 1620.

SECTION

8

ABOUT
ROBERT H. SCHULLER

Robert H. Schuller is one of the most widely known churchmen in America today. He is the founder-pastor of the world's first walk-in, drive-in inspiration center. However, he is much more.

He is an author, lecturer, a newspaper columnist, a television personality. The message of "Possibility Thinking" he propounds has brought inspiration and peace of mind to peoples around the world. As a result he is one of the most dynamic and electric men in the world today.

His base is the Garden Grove, California, Community Church. Each Sunday, his television program, "Hour of Power" is seen by millions of devoted followers in every state of the union, Canada and Australia—on over 165 stations. The program is also carried around the world on the Armed Forces network.

Dr. Schuller arrived in California from Iowa in 1955 with just $500. He persuaded a drive-in theater owner to let him speak there on Sunday mornings, delivering his first sermon from the roof of the theater snack bar to scattered families seated in 50 cars.

Dr. Schuller's reputation grew speedily. Today, his church is a graceful, 14-story landmark, with 10 full-time ministers assisting in the work. Each Sunday, over 8,000 people converge on the tranquil 22-acre campus to hear his inspiring messages, some sitting in their cars, some sitting in chairs on the lawn, some sitting in the pews of this ultra-modern edifice.

Later, the nationally televised ministry, Hour of Power, was begun and Dr. Schuller's uplifting philosophy began to spread. A passionate exponent of the sovereignty of the individual vs. the collectivist state, he speaks on that subject in the introductory pages which follow.

THE RIGHT TO THE REALIZATION OF THE AMERICAN DREAM—SOVEREIGNTY OF THE INDIVIDUAL UNDER GOD

By ROBERT H. SCHULLER

In all of history, no dream has exercised so powerful a hold on the human spirit as the American Dream. Basic to that dream is the right of each individual to soar as high as his God-given talents and abilities will take him.

Two hundred years ago, a band of patriots convened in Philadelphia to undertake what appeared to be an impossible task—to rid three million people of the domination of a king over their lives. I am certain they faced the ridicule of those negative thinkers who predicted failure and defeat. There are always those dreary impossibility thinkers who deluge us with cynical, gloomy, pessimistic predictions. But these founding fathers were driven by a dream —that a nation could be founded on the principle "that all men are created equal, that they are endowed by their Creator with certain unalienable rights, that among these are life, liberty and the pursuit of happiness."

These "first citizens" were a motley group of foreigners. They did not even speak the same language. Some spoke English, others spoke Dutch, German, Spanish or French. Later on they were joined by the Irish, Italians, Hungarians, Russians and Polish. Then came the Chinese, Japanese and Mexican. All were driven to these shores by the dream that an individual has certain unalienable rights. Each man and each woman is sovereign under God! That is a basic right!

But hardly had they achieved nationhood when the bowels of our land were torn and ripped by a ghastly civil war—neighbor against neighbor, father against son.

But we survived! And soon, covered wagons gave way to railroads, the railroads were joined by highways and then by giant jet airlines streaking across the skies. During this time, other wars came, along with violent changes in the economy which led to the Great Depression, soup lines and suicides. Yet somehow, through the years, a deep faith surged from the very depth of this country's soul. America not only survived, it grew.

How? Why? What has kept this amalgamation of people standing firm through these invincible two hundred years? Where did the courage come from? Where did the faith and endurance originate? In 1776, Thomas Paine wrote: "What we obtain too cheaply, we esteem too lightly. It is dearness only that gives everything its value. Heaven knows how to put a price upon its goods, and it would be strange indeed if so celestial an article as freedom should not be highly rated."

No country knows greater freedom than our country. Freedom to choose our life's work, to travel from state to state without border guards. The freedom to try and succeed; to try and fail and yet not be put in prison for failure. We enjoy the freedom to speak, write, praise, question or criticize anyone, no matter how high his station or rank, and not fear a knock on the door in the middle of the night. The freedom to start our own business and become a capitalist, building a fortune, creating dignified job opportunities and new products for the betterment of life. We enjoy the freedom to be proud, confident, and bold. We can do anything, climb any mountain and achieve any objective. Possibilities are unlimited!

Sovereignty of the individual is the basic ingredient of the American success formula. It is the mainspring of human progress. For countless centuries it has been cherished by man, but only in America has it been truly established!

But as we dream our dreams and dare to believe, we must also be on guard. Woodrow Wilson cautioned that "the history of liberty is a history of the limitation of governmental power, not the increase of it. When we resist concentration of power, we are resisting the processes of death, because concentration of power is what always preceded the destruction of human liberties."

It was our founding father's passionate belief in the rights and the responsibility of the individual to determine his own destiny that gave birth to America. For two centuries we have been witnesses to the world that a people could structure a caste-free republic that offered to all an equal opportunity to pursue life's rewards, each according to his own choice and his own will to earn these benefits. But we will only remain such a nation by holding fast to the disciplines that molded us—self-reliance, the character to each solve his own problems,

doing without that which we cannot pay for, and the self-respect earned only through self-dependence.

I believe it is possible for us to bring about a "rebirth" of our nation as it begins its third century. I see our unquenchable, indestructible, imperishable spirit of human freedom spreading to the uttermost part of the world. As we rededicate ourselves to the sovereignty of the individual—a creed that forged us and created the greatest system of self-government, freedom and abundance that mankind has ever known—we will see the fulfillment of the prayer we have been singing for years:

> "Not for this land alone,
>   but be God's mercies shown,
>   from shore to shore,
>   And may the nations see,
>   that men should brothers be,
>   and form one family,
>   the wide world o'er."

Freedom under God expands our horizons, stimulates our imagination, releases creative energies, accelerates our progress and fosters our personal fulfillment. Thomas Jefferson reminded us that "the God who gave us life, gave us liberty." The liberties of a nation can only be secure when we have a continuing and growing conviction that these liberties are the gift of God.

As I prepare myself for our country's third century, my prayer is,
"Our fathers' God to Thee, author of liberty, to thee we sing.
Long may our land be bright with freedom's holy light.
Protect us by thy might, great God, our King."

Robert Schuller

This woodcut illustrates the first known national flag, which was the result of the now famous flag resolution of June 3, 1777, written almost a year after the declaration of Independence:

"Resolved: that the flag of the United States of America be 13 stripes alternate red and white, that the union be 13 stars, white in a blue field representing a new constellation."

This short sentence announced a happening compared to which all American historical episodes seem dwarfed.

Woodcut by M. Welman

Out of the flesh, out of the minds and hearts
Of thousands upon thousand common men,
Cranks, martyrs, starry-eyed enthusiasts,
Slow-spoken neighbors, hard to push around,
Women whose hands were gentle with their kids
And men with a cold passion for mere justice,
We made this thing, this dream.

         — Stephen Vincent Benet

"They had no word for crisis — only danger and opportunity"

WHEN America was a young creative nation, our language did not include the word "crisis." Instead we used two words — *danger* and *opportunity*.

Might be a good rule for our country today.

There is a grave *danger* of ruinous inflation, yet *opportunity* to stop it by producing more value for everything we receive.

There is danger of overwhelming federal debt, yet opportunity to control and reduce it by asking less of government and doing more things for ourselves.

There is danger abroad, yet opportunity to strengthen our defenses by listening to our experts and respecting them for the fine patriots they are.

All the traits and human resources which made this nation great are still here, but obscured by a selfishness which has made too many cry for something for nothing. And that *has* brought a crisis but one which can still be met by recognizing those dangers and grasping the opportunity to return to *work* in true American character.

Daniel Boone escorting settlers through the Cumberland Gap
By George Caleb Bingham. Courtesy, Washington University Gallery of Art

Where is that country we used to know?

IN THE America of yesterday you paid your debts as quickly as possible, and went without things to do it.

You disciplined your children — but disciplined yourself first.

You spent less than you earned, and demanded your governments do the same.

You went to church, your children to Sunday School, you held daily prayers — and no court would have dared to interpose any law into your private religion.

You would have been horrified at (and quick to change) men in high places who made "deals."

You expected to prosper only by doing a better and better job.

You obeyed the law — but took active enough part in government to see that the laws were just.

You "walked softly but carried a big stick."

And *that* was the *character* which brought this country victory in three wars in your lifetime, built it back from a shattering depression, and fed and saved the civilized world.

Have a little fun for a change – you deserve it

SURE, gasoline is higher priced. But you can still drive, and every average American family has a car. That's true in no other nation on earth.

Yes, prices are high, but food is in amply supply and meat is probably on your regular diet. True almost nowhere else.

Our banks and insurance companies are solvent. Almost 100% of our police, teachers, military are loyal Americans. You can still vote freely for the officials of your choice.

There are more Americans at work and for higher pay than ever before.

Of course we have serious problems — we always have had. But we've always had the courage and stamina to work out of them.

Gloom never got you anywhere. Let's get back to enjoying life again.

There can be no freedom of the individual, no democracy, without the capital system. These are, in the end, inseparable. Those who would destroy freedom have only first to destroy the hope of gain, the profit motive of enterprise and risk taking, the hope of accumulating capital, the hope to save something for one's old age and for one's children. For a community of men without property, and without hope of getting it by honest efforts, is a community of slaves of a despotic state."

— Russell C. Leffingwell.